12-31-73

**Two Democratic Labor
Leaders in Conflict**

Two Democratic Labor Leaders in Conflict

The Latin American Revolution and the Role of the Workers

Carroll Hawkins
Michigan State University

Lexington Books
D.C. Heath and Company
Lexington, Massachusetts
Toronto   London

Library of Congress Cataloging in Publication Data

Hawkins, Carroll, 1910-
  Two democratic leaders in conflict.

  Bibliography: p.
  1. Trade unions–Latin America. 2. Jáuregui, Arturo. 3. Máspero,
Emilio. I. Title.
HD6530.5.H39   331.88'098   73-1008
ISBN 0-669-86678-4

Copyright © 1973 by D.C. Heath and Company.

Published simultaneously in Canada.

Printed in the United States of America.

International Standard Book Number: 0-669-86678-4

Library of Congress Catalog Card Number: 73-1008

**In very different ways for the
CH's—the two Charlies—
and** *La Margarita*

1784384

Contents

Key to Agencies, Unions, and Union Affiliates

FAT, Frente Autentico del Trabajo
ORIT, Organizacion Regional Inter-americana de Trabajadores
CLASC (now CLAT), Confederacion Latino Americana de Sindicalistas Cristianas
ILO, International Labor Office
AFL-CIO, American Federation of Labor-Congress of Industrial Organizations
AIFLD, American Institute for Free Labor Development
ICFTU, International Confederation of Free Trade Unions
WCL, World Confederation of Labor
JOC, Juventud Obrera Catolica
ASA, Associacion Sindical Argentina
INES, Instituto Nacional de Estudios Sindicales
WFTU, World Federation of Trade Unions
FCL, Frente Campesino Latino
CTP, Confederacion de Trabajadores del Peru
CGT, Confederacion General de Trabajadores (Argentina)
IFDC, Instituto de Formacion Democrata Cristiana
APRA, Alianza Popular Revolucionaria Americana
CTAL, Confederacion de Trabajadores de America Latina
CIT, Confederacion Inter-americana de Trabajadores
CTV, Confederacion de Trabajadores de Venezuela
CUTCH, Central Unica de Trabajadores de Chile
CTM, Confederacion de Trabajadores de Mexico
CLAT, Central Latino Americana de Trabajadores
PRI, Partido Revolucionario Institucional
CUT, Confederacion Unificada de Trabajadores
CASC, Confederacion Autónomo de Sindicalistas Cristianas
Confederacion Nacion–CASC, Confederacion Autónomo de Sindicalistas Cristianas
CNTL (CONATRAL), Al De Trabajadores (República Dominicana)
CTC, Confederacion de Trabajadores de Cuba
*COSATE, Trade Union Technical Advisory Committee (OAS)
*COTPAL, The Permanent Technical Committee on Labor Matters (OAS)
OAS, Organization of American States
IFCTU, International Federation of Christian Trade Unions
*CPUSTAL, The Permanent Latin American Trade Union Congress

---

*Author's note: I have only been able to find English spelling. Obviously letters refer to Spanish titles.

Acknowledgments

Six months research done mainly in Chile and Mexico (which began a study of many years in many different places) was partially financed by a grant from the Michigan State University Latin American Studies Center. A grant from the American Philosophical Society aided later in the completion of the research done in Europe. The author also wishes to thank the numerous persons in Latin America, Europe, and the United States who assisted in the making of this study. These include high- and low-level labor officials, members of embassies (especially British and American), clergymen, scholars, businessmen, specialists, members of political parties, of government ministries, of private foundations, rank and file trade unionists, political exiles, journalists, informed hangers-on, barbers, and chauffeurs. The principal Latin American centers visited were Santiago, Valparaiso, Lima, Mexico City, Monterrey, Buenos Aires, and San José. In Europe, Brussels, Bonn, Frankfurt, Paris, and Geneva furnished the main opportunities for research. Some time was also spent in Washington, D.C.

Special thanks are due to the following: Members of the ORIT staff in Mexico City and Cuernavaca; CLASC (now CLAT) officials in Santiago in 1967; leaders of the Mexican-affiliate of CLAT the FAT; former and present officials of the (then) International Federation of Christian Trade Unions, (now) the World Confederation of Labor in the Brussels headquarters; officials of the International Confederation of Free Trade Unions, also in Brussels; Specialists in the ILO, as well as trade union officials of labor international confederations located in Geneva; Latin American specialists of the AFL-CIO and the AIFLD; and to José Rangel Parra.

Professor Garland Wood, former director of Michigan State University's Latin American Studies Center, first encouraged the author to undertake the research and helped later to sustain him in the face of various problems to its completion. Professor John Hunter, the present director of the Center, read the draft manuscript, made suggestions, and arranged for the typing. Professors William Faunce, former director of research in the School of Labor and Industrial Relations, M.S.U., and Albert Blum of the School, were particularly helpful. Mrs. Jane Green typed the last draft. I, of course, am responsible for the interpretations of the data to the gathering of which so many contributed.

**Two Democratic Labor
Leaders in Conflict**

1 Introduction

In Latin America today the main organizational protagonists in a hemispheric contest for the loyalties of the urban and rural worker continue to be the ORIT and the former CLASC (now renamed the CLAT). For the past decade that conflict has in a great measure been shaped by the views of the present secretaries general of the two organizations, Arturo Jáuregui of the ORIT and Emilio Máspero of the CLAT.

Both the much larger *Organización Regional Inter-Americana de Trabajadores* and its rival, the *Central Latino Americana de Trabajadores*, are avowedly non-Communist, democratic workers groupings. The ORIT officials, when in an expansive mood, claim a membership of some thirty millions. As its title indicates, the ORIT is an inter-American body. About one-half of its members are from the United States and Canada. The CLAT adherents, who may be inclined to be even more exaggerated in their figures particularly since the renaming of their previous organization in November 1971, claim some five million members, all of whom are *latinos*. The CLAT is emphatically proud of its purely Latin American nature.[a]

The two have carried on a continuing and intensifying rivalry since the founding of the CLAT's predecessor, the CLASC, in 1954 in Santiago some three years after the origin of ORIT in Mexico. Acrimony and argument are carried by the leaders to the highest labor councils of the United States, Canada, and Europe. Arturo Jáuregui and Emilio Máspero in recent years have been the elected officials who are mainly responsible for shaping the nature of the conflict as it exists today. The ORIT with its more pragmatic stance—its efforts to create, develop, and sustain trade unions, emphasizing methods and goals which reflect the experience of trade unionism in the advanced western countries, especially in the United States and Canada and the populist politics of the Latin American milieu—reveals the influence of Jáuregui, the experienced diplomatic, good labor bureaucrat. The more charismatic, dynamic personality of Máspero, with the ceaseless energy of the social revolutionist, was earlier reflected in the more ideological "missionary" character of the CLASC. This revolutionary militancy is now carried further in the message Máspero has presented to the CLAT.

[a]From 1954 until late 1971 the predecessor to the CLAT was the CLASC, the CONFEDERACION LATINO AMERICANA DE SINDICALISMO CRISTIANO, the Latin American Confederation of Christian Trade Unions. CLAT, the Latin American Workers Central, like the former CLASC, is the regional organization of the world labor body, the World Confederation of Labor. The reasons for the change in name and the implications of the change are discussed below.

1

It was when Máspero first became an organizer for the CLASC in 1960 that the aggressive stance of the Christian organization began to emerge. From the start he overshadowed the mild Chilean José ("Pepe") Goldsack whom he replaced as president in October 1966. Jáuregui's rise in a more viable organization was less meteoric but no less significant. When he became Secretary General of the ORIT in 1961 he had already held the office of Acting Secretary General during Secretary General Luis Alberto Mongé's extended leave of absence following the 1955 ORIT hemispheric convention.

Máspero and Jáuregui share the common characteristic which students of labor in developing areas find somewhat rare—they are in their personal lives *hombres limpios*, "clean uncorruptible men" who are truly dedicated to their respective organizations. Pro-democratic and "clean" they disagree on fundamental questions—on the primary function of the trade union movement in Latin America today, on the type of unionism that should be built within the Latin American society of the future, on the nature of outside assistance to Latin American unions and the type of outsiders with which those relations are made. Most importantly, while each endorses the need for a Latin American social revolution, each sees the nature of that radical change differently and also follows a different road to reach the revolutionary goal.[1]

The main arguments of these dissenting leaders are of single importance. They directly relate to programs and overt actions of the United States government and the interests of certain European governments in the Latin American labor scene. They reveal the considerable involvement of organized labor in the United States and in Europe in matters of labor and politics in the southern part of the Western Hemisphere. They are deeply concerned with the challenge of communism throughout Latin America while at the same time they reveal decidedly different approaches to dealing with that challenge. And again it should be underscored that they reflect two contrasting views concerning the way necessary change should be secured. Máspero aims at a revolution largely secured through attacking the present political order. Jáuregui believes in a kind of "revolution through evolution" within the Latin American political milieu.

These arguments, moreover, occur in a world in which underdeveloped areas are assessing their contacts and experiences with the older established orders such as the United States and the "matured" Soviet Union. Underdeveloped Latin America is seeking an independent course leaning more to the "Third World" position. Jáuregui and Máspero both assert their basic independence but they have different ideas as to how best to really achieve that independence.

This book will examine the nature and the roots of the disagreements between the two labor *jefes* endeavoring to do justice to each presentation and seeking to explain why each protagonist developed his particular perspective. Some conclusions will be offered concerning the strengths and weaknesses in the arguments of each leader and of their respective organizations at this time. Not the least of the burdens imposed here will be that of assessing how important the

ORIT and the CLAT really are, judging the impact of the personality of each leader upon his particular organization, and the effectiveness of his messages in the contemporary Latin American *ambiente*.

Some students regard the ORIT and the CLAT as little more than agencies of corporate bodies located outside Latin America. These foreign centers are the United States in the case of the ORIT, and Europe in the case of the CLAT. The precise nature of the relationship between the two organizations and their foreign benefactors, however, is unclear. The two labor leaders strongly disagree over the nature of the relationship, as well as over just *who* the foreign supporters are.

It is generally agreed by students of the matter that each leader depends upon sources outside of Latin America for a great deal of the finances which permit him to conduct his operations. Each has foreign benefactors including national union organizations and union international bodies and governments which directly or indirectly support him. Máspero also benefits from part of the monies collected under the auspices of European Catholic clergy for general welfare and educational purposes abroad. These wellsprings of sustenance are for the ORIT chiefly located in the United States and for the CLASC mainly in Europe.[2]

From various knowledgeable parties in Washington, Mexico City, Santiago, Caracas, Bonn, Brussels, and Geneva, the researcher will obtain different figures as to the amounts of money received and expended by each labor grouping. Each leader dwells upon the greater largesse bestowed on the opposition by its particular foreign supporters. ORIT sources repeatedly informed me in Mexico City and elsewhere that the CLASC (now CLAT) coffers are much more generously laden with foreign monies than are its own. And sitting at an excellent lunch in Brussels as the guest of one of the most important European figures in channeling monies to Máspero's organization, I was told: "Our investment in Latin America is exceedingly small in comparison to that of the Americans and we believe we are getting a far greater return for it than they are."[3]

The bulk of the ORIT income according to various observers comes from the AFL-CIO, the United States government, and the International Solidarity Fund of the parent body, the International Confederation of Free Trade Unions, ICFTU. Some perhaps is indirectly received from American business corporations. This latter would come from those corporations who support the American Institute for Free Labor Development (AIFLD). This is the AFL-CIO Latin American educational and social works agency established in 1962, which itself has received considerable financial support from the United States government.[4]

There is a very close relationship between the AFL-CIO, the American Institute for Free Labor Development, and the ORIT. Senior officers of the AFL-CIO are members of the ORIT. They represent the most powerful affiliate of the hemispheric organization. AFL-CIO personnel have served as assistant secretaries-general with their offices in the ORIT headquarters at Mexico City. Arturo Jáuregui is, in turn, a member of the AIFLD governing board. William C. Doherty, Jr., an experienced Latin Americanist, the present executive director of the AIFLD, has been featured at numerous ORIT meetings and has at time served as an ORIT spokesman at scholarly conferences dealing with Latin America. Relations between AIFLD staff and ORIT staff are close and continuous all over Latin America.[5]

The AFL-CIO is a primary agency in formally channeling financial assistance to the ORIT through its assessments as the most affluent member of the inter-American labor organization. It advises Washington on what it sees as labor's interests in Latin America and requests governmental financial backing in the support of these interests. Under such circumstances it is not strange that the ORIT is regarded with favor by the United States Department of State. AFL-CIO leaders also initiated the idea that "progressive American business corporations" involve themselves (through the AIFLD) with Latin American trade union development. The American labor body (again, as the richest) was the heaviest contributor to the Solidarity Fund of the world organization, the International Confederation of Free Trade Unions until its withdrawal from the ICFTU in February 1969. The ICFTU itself, as a world organization, has an interest in Latin America, but the AFL-CIO during its years of membership in the ICFTU was permitted a virtual carte blanche in that area of the world.[6]

In contrast to the ORIT, the CLAT receives the greatest share of its funding from European sources. These include the Solidarity Fund of the World Confederation of Labor (WCL); the German Christian Foundation; International Solidarity; and a private foundation mainly organized by a leading European Christian trade union figure. One of the main supporters of the CLAT that is frequently mentioned is what has been called the "German Bishop's Fund" for various charitable, educational, and other more specific eleemosynary purposes. The *Reporter* magazine of February 25, 1965 carried a story in which a great deal was made of the help given to the then CLASC by the German bishops. The writer of that article was probably referring to *Misererum*, a German Catholic enterprise directed by the Cardinal of Cologne. I have been told by informed Americans working in Europe as well as by Europeans, that a varying share of such clerical sponsored monies goes to the WCL International Solidarity Fund and in this manner finds its way to the Latin American affiliate. Members of the Catholic clergy interviewed in Germany and Belgium during the summer of 1967 asserted that no money went directly to the CLASC, but that funds did go for charitable and educational purposes throughout the world including Latin America. A scholarly priest, a Latin American specialist, explained that there exists a committee of clergy and laymen who advise on the matter of allocating these monies to various "worthy" enterprises all over the world. Included in this advisory committee has been a prestigious figure of the international Christian trade union organizations. CLASC officials and their friends repeatedly told me that any funds raised by German clergy have been used in Latin America strictly for "educational and charitable" purposes.

The German government itself has been reported as indirectly contributing to the CLASC, but there have been repeated denials of this. However, the Konrad Adenauer *Stifdung*, a German Christian foundation, is the recipient of governmental funds, some of which are allotted to Latin America in its general budget.[7]

This foreign assistance to the ORIT and the CLASC is important. So important that to some students it suggests that the true contestants exist behind-the-scenes and are not Latin Americans.[8] Jáuregui and Máspero have periodically feuded over this matter with each dwelling upon the evils that are apparent to him in the other's receipt of foreign assistance while at the same time explaining and justifying what are said to be limited funds that each claims to receive from outside benefactors. Each accuses the other of being greatly influenced or controlled by external agencies due to his dependence on them for financial support.

Although foreign monies may be crucial to the operations of both the CLAT and the ORIT the position taken here is that this makes them no more the simple tools of their benefactors than Fidel Castro, for example, is the tool of his benefactors the Soviet Union. The two rival democratic labor leaders have at times (as has Castro, of whom they are critical) exhibited their independence of their foreign benefactors. Although they are on most issues in basic agreement with those who supply financial funds, Jáuregui and Máspero are not without the important resources that arise mainly from their hold upon their fellow Latin American workers. As *latinos* they can draw upon this relationship for support when they desire to remind their foreign friends that their cooperative activities are presumed to be primarily for the benefit of the Latin American workers.

Emilio Máspero

Emilio Máspero was born in Argentina in 1930, the son of Italian immigrants. His formal education was terminated very early after he had spent some time in an Argentine Jesuit novitiate.[9] He had to start work at a very early age, beginning as a bellboy in the same hotel where his father worked as a waiter. Subsequently he worked in a law office, a textile factory, and eventually in the metallurgical industry as a lathe mechanic. Thus from his twelfth year he was well acquainted with the rigors of hard work. Máspero, however, did not spend any great part of his early life among the workers at the shop level. For he was soon caught up in the work of the J.O.C. (*Juventud Obrera Católica*), the Latin American branch of a worldwide organization of young Catholic workers. Through it he became intimately acquainted with the various elements of international Christian trade unions prior to the formation of the CLASC in 1954.[10]

At the age of twenty-two, Máspero was elected president of the Argentine J.O.C. Later he was chosen the J.O.C. representative for all of South America at its 1952 convention held in Petrópolis, Brazil. By 1955, working through the J.O.C. he was a main figure in the creation of ASA (*Asociación Sindical Argentina*), a Christian trade union group through which he sought to combat the influence of Peronism. Peronism affected the Argentine workers then, as it does today, even though Juan Peron, the former dictator, had gone into exile.[11] Máspero's audacity aimed at nothing less than infiltrating the powerful *Peronista* labor body, the General Confederation of Workers, CGT. Young Máspero's rise through the auspices of the J.O.C. also provided him with an opportunity to study and travel in Europe. A scholarship from a Catholic organization, *Pax Christi*, sent him abroad in 1957. The scholarship was for three months, but he remained a full year traveling, working, writing, and speaking as he moved among the humble and the great in the Christian worker circles in most of the countries of Western Europe and Spain. It was during this time that his forceful personality and brilliance first made an impact upon the elite of the European Christian trade union movement and their spiritual supporters in the clergy. In the impassioned, nationalistic Argentinian they saw a young dynamic figure who could spark their initial drive among the Latin American workers which had begun just three years earlier under the direction of the Chilean, José Goldsack.

Máspero returned to Argentina reassured by his contacts with the European Christian Left and Center. In 1960, he became CLASC's first permanent organizer in Latin America. His base of operations was Carácas where he held the office of executive secretary for the Caribbean area of the CLASC. His career as a CLASC officer was now in flower and it carried him to further renown. From his Venezuelan center he developed as a truly powerful figure within the Christian labor world. He was not only an executive secretary and hemispheric organizer, but also a labor educator—a professor in the National Institute of Labor Studies (INES) and in the Institute of Democratic Christian Formation (IFDC), both located in Venezuela. In his activities in his assigned area, the Caribbean zone, his travel in the United States where he met AFL-CIO leaders, (he was irked by some, but impressed by Walter Reuther), his lectures at universities in Latin America and the United States, in conferences of Christian trade union leaders in Latin America and Europe, the young Argentinian, now of Carácas, showed the labor world that he was a rising figure of great potential.

Already Máspero, as a good *político*, had begun to assemble his own group within the CLASC, eventually to gain him in the fall of 1966 the secretary general's office.[12] At the same time his independent mind made him a controversial figure. He openly avowed his conception of left-wing Christianity. Some important adherents of the international Christian labor movement in Latin America and throughout the world labeled him "anti-church," "overly ambitious," "extremist," and "somewhat dangerous."

The U.S. Department of State, the AFL-CIO, and the ORIT now began to be concerned with what they came to regard as a brash young anti-American devisive upstart. For years CLASC had been treated by the Americans with disdain. Now they increasingly took more notice of the stinging "little fly" and his small organization.

In the Panama Congress of CLASC, in October 1966, Máspero's team swept into office and without any controversy Goldsack bowed to the inevitable. At the age of thirty-six, Emilio Máspero had confirmed by office what had increasingly been apparent in the years prior to his election, the fact that he was indeed the true leader of the CLASC. He was now in a position to make his policies even better known throughout international labor circles and the capitals of the world.

Arturo Jáuregui

Máspero's rival, Arturo Jáuregui, is also comparatively young, although he is some ten years older than the CLASC leader. He was born in Lima in 1920, the son of a taxi driver and a seamstress. After finishing his high school education (divided between *el Colegio Modelo* and *la Escuela Técnica de Comercio*), he took evening courses in the social sciences at the Catholic University. From boyhood he had always been interested in learning, and over the years he continued intermittently to pursue (mostly informally) social science studies, especially those concerned with labor economics and politics, in universities in Mexico, Chile, and Brazil, among others.[13]

A the age of sixteen, Jáuregui became a worker in the *Alianza* factory in Lima, which made noodles and pasta for the *La Fabril* company. In the six years he spent in the factory he took an active role in asserting workers' grievances and constructively seeking to improve working conditions. He helped to organize the factory union which was founded at the time and he subsequently devoted himself to championing its cause in a variety of ways, chiefly political.

During this time, between his sixteenth and twenty-second years, Jáuregui had come under the influence of Raúl Haya de la Torre and the *Aprista* movement which Haya had founded in exile in Mexico in 1931. The *Apristas* were a highly nationalistic, Indo-latino, non-Communist, semi-Marxist party of intellectuals, students, and workers. From boyhood Jáuregui had known the story of the previous years of work, persecution, and exile that the youthful Haya de la Torre and the students had experienced in their support of Peruvian trade unionism. When he joined the *Aprista* Youth in 1936 at the age of sixteen he was a thoroughly infatuated convert. The Peruvian government frequently persecuted and harassed labor leaders, particularly *Apristas*. Later Jáuregui would know imprisonment and exile.[14]

In the story of Peruvian up-and-down politics, the years of José Luís Bustamante's presidency (1945-1948) were singularly favorable for trade unionism and the APRA, itself, which had supported Bustamente's candidacy. But in his last months in office the president, returning to the more familiar ways, outlawed the APRA because some of its leaders had become his critics. It was during these years that Jáuregui began his early career as a labor official. In 1945, he was elected secretary general of another union which he helped to found in the Sidney Ross soap factory. The following year his active part in the First National Congress of Peruvian Employees, held in Lima, led to his being elected Organizing Secretary of the General Federation of Employees. In this office he traveled extensively throughout Peru and became increasingly known to labor people all over the country. From 1946 to 1948 (from the age of twenty-six to twenty-eight), he was the Federation's representative to Peru's national labor organization, the *Confederaciń de Trabajadores Peruanos* (CTP). During these years he was also a member of the National Executive Committee of that body.

By 1948, with the cold war on the horizon, a movement developed throughout Latin America for the formation of a non-Communist, inter-American labor organization. Non-Communist Latin American trade union leaders by this time had become unhappy, or suspicious, concerning the existing Latin American regional labor body, the *Confederacion de Trabajadores América Latina* (CTAL). Originally a genuine liberal-left coalition, when founded in 1936, the CTAL had subsequently developed under the brilliant Mexican Marxist, Lombardo Toledano, into a Communist transmission belt, i.e., a nominally non-Communist group that was an agency for Communist-approved ideas. The dissenting Latin American trade unions which now sought to form a new hemispheric agency included some like the Peruvians—who were affiliated with the CTAL—and other newer outside militant organizations in Costa Rica, Venezuela, and Colombia who were strongly opposed to communism.

Of seminal importance at the time was the decision of the American Federation of Labor (after some twenty years of comparative neglect of Latin America) to again actively enter the area. Its principal spokesman in Latin America, Italian-born, former socialist Serafino Romualdi, had in 1946 been appointed AFL Latin American representative. With Romualdi's help the anti-Communist and/or non-Communist elements together with the AFL and the Canadian Trades and Labor Council formed a new inter-American labor body, the *Confederación Interamericano de Trabajadores*, (CIT). Its founding congress was held in Lima in January 1948.

Events in the world of international labor politics were moving rapidly. The World Federation of Trade Unions, a labor international group formed by the leading Western and Communist labor movements of 1946 in the spirit of hope resulting from the wartime alliance, had by 1949 split apart. The Western non-Communist affiliates withdrew charging that the WFTU had become a Communist front. They quickly set about forming a new international body, now joined by the American Federation of Labor which, unlike the American

CIO, had refused to be a part of the WFTU. Thus the present International Confederation of Free Trade Unions was established in 1949 with the AFL and the CIO joining with the principal national union organizations of the western world in its creation.

In the Western Hemisphere the CIT, as might be expected, reacted to the events in Europe. At its second Congress it moved to provide for its own demise if its leaders could link up with the new big Western world grouping. The ICFTU leadership was friendly to the overtures and in January 1951 in Mexico City a new inter-American organization, containing most of the former CIT union groupings, the present ORIT—the Western hemispheric affiliate of the ICFTU— was created.[15]

On the Latin American scene the youthful Arturo Jáuregui actively participated in all of these activities. He was a main figure in the formation of the CIT and its evolution to the ORIT. Secretary-treasurer of the short-lived CIT, he later occupied various top administrative posts in the central headquarters of the ORIT (including that of acting general secretary) until 1958 when he returned to Peru to work in the labor movement of his native country. In 1961 at the Fifth ORIT Congress held in Brazil he was recalled and elected to his present position as secretary general.

In his way to the top Jáuregui has been aided by his own comrades of the early days, some of whom were traditionalistic Latin American socialists. They were experienced labor leaders, veterans of scores of battles with Communists, oligarchs of industry and government, cryptofascists, the military and conservative church elements—that panoply against which these comparatively young leaders had to struggle. Like Jáuregui they share a major concern with communism as a primary threat to labor. They include Bernardo Ibañez, former president of the CIT and the first director of the ORIT's school for worker's education located in Cuernavaca, Mexico.

Jáuregui's earlier radical *Aprismo* beliefs have softened in accordance with the recent interpretations of Haya de la Torre. To this day, however, two of the original elements of *Aprismo*, its anti-communism, and its assertation of the primacy of Latin American goals, have affected the ORIT leader's general stance. Of the four ORIT's secretaries-general, he has been the most outspoken and wide-ranging in condemning Communists.[16] Under the sting of charges that he is controlled by AFL-CIO influence he has periodically publicly reiterated that it must be remembered that Latin Americans, too, were the originators of the activities which culminated in forming the CIT and soon after the ORIT. At the same time, along with the older *Apristas*, Jáuregui has long since recanted his earlier belief that Yankee imperialism is Latin America's main danger. He now believes in cooperation with friendly Americans from the North on a basis of mutual respect. This and his firm anti-Communist record undoubtedly contributed to his rise to power in the ORIT, whose most powerful affiliate is George Meany's AFL-CIO. It should also be recalled, however, that in addition to Jáuregui for the most part the Latin American participants in the founding of the ORIT were themselves fervent anti-Communists.

Periodically revealed in his conflict with the CLASC (now CLAT) is another *Aprista* heritage—anti-clericalism. Jáuregui, a practicing Catholic from his youth, has fervently believed in the utter separation of the Church from trade union affairs. He accepts, however, what he sees as progressive Catholic but non-Church influence in trade unions. He approved, for example, of the Catholic-inspired Colombian *Union de Trabajadores de Colombia* and the *Confederación Costaricense del Trabajo Rerum Novarum* of Costa Rica, along with the strongly Catholic-oriented Christian Democratic members within the Venezuelan CTV. All of these are affiliates of the ORIT. He is, however, an enemy of "confessionalism" in any guise and he repeatedly charges that Máspero is an "ex-seminarian" who acts to keep labor within bounds shaped implicitly by the Catholic Church and by the Christian Democratic parties.

Máspero denies the charge asserting that his organization is in no way controlled by the Catholic Church or Catholic action groups, that there is no religious or ecclesiastical discrimination within what was formerly Christian trade unionism and that the term "Christian" referred to a social philosophy or ethic which appeals to all men of good will. The change of the CLASC to the CLAT has been accompanied by Máspero's further declaration of independence from Church influence and severe judgments of the Church's relations to the workers of Latin America. To Jáuregui's charges of "confessionalism" Máspero counterattacks by charging that Jáuregui and the ORIT lack a social philosophy and moral character, that they perform in accordance with the pressure from the AFL-CIO and the U.S. Department of State. In other words, Máspero says that, at bottom, Jáuregui is an agent of Yankee imperialism working within Latin American labor circles. The two rival chieftans regard each other and the organizations they lead with suspicion and disdain which at times gives the impression that the raison d'être for the existence of their respective groupings is the recruitment of partisans.

The acrimonious conflict, however, reflects much more than a personal cold war fueled by behind-the-scenes partisan powerful foreign benefactors. Far more important than the personal bitterness is the consequences which the conflict has upon an understanding of the proceedings for change and for the success of the social revolution which each leader avows he is supporting. These avowals have been reiterated by Jáuregui and Máspero in innumerable public speeches, in the press, and from the platforms of labor congresses all over the world. Jáuregui is well aware that his critics regard him and his organization as agents of North American obstructionism—as really being counterrevolutionary. He flatly rejects this charge and asserts that in the end it will be seen that he proved to be the more effective instrumentalist in bringing about social change. Máspero scorns the pragmatic "bread and butter" philosophy of the ORIT which he sees as the consequence of its Yankee domination. The North Americans through the ORIT, he believes, are really obstructing the needed social revolution.

Before elaborating the conflicting perspectives of the protagonists let us briefly survey the social environment of the vast stage upon which the labor drama is currently being portrayed.

2 The Setting

Latin America comprises a vast area of different countries in different stages of nationhood and with a growing populist nationalism, suffering for the most part from the common ills arising from extremes of poverty and wealth. It is a social order with a feudal early history. The interpersonal relationships of that history, those of a highly stratified society, have made their mark upon twentieth century Latin America. While industrialization has contributed in different ways to the overall improvement of the lives of many Latin Americans and has even given some hope for the further progressive development of the area as a whole, it has also brought innumerable problems, some similar to those arising in Europe in the early decades of the Industrial Revolution and others complicated by the particular social, economic, and political ambiente of the Latin American society. Indeed, in the long run, the overall consequences of industrialization might be negative for developing a democratic politics unless significant changes which go to the roots of the political and social structure are made. With all the problems arising from industrialization and increasingly rapid urbanization, the countryside, the center of approximately one-half of the entire Latin American working force, in many ways constitutes a major, if not *the* fundamental, problem today.[1]

In Latin America, moreover, there are vast problems of disease, the most rapidly increasing population rate in the world as well as economic discrepancies and backward agricultural practices. These principally affect those whom Jáuregui and Máspero seek to guide—the masses of workers.

Trade union growth and development in the area reveals wide diversities between different countries. While many unions principally located in Argentina, Uruguay, Chile, Mexico, and Brazil can stand comparison with those in other countries of the western world outside Latin America, in general Latin American unions have only primitive development, are financially poor, and poorly organized and disciplined.

There are innumerable factors which further contribute to the overall underdevelopment and affect unions negatively—the still limited nature of the economies, too much production of and dependence upon agricultural products, the semifeudal relations of workers and managers, particularly in the country-side, the continuing paternalism (often characterizing the urban factory conditions), as well as the vast discrepancy of resources and status between unions within the same countries so that there are elite groups who form a labor aristocracy alongside others that are of the most primitive kind. Of seminal

13

importance is the fact that freedom of association is often lacking in practice no matter what the laws provide. The appalling illiteracy of the masses of people in most countries, the suspicion and antagonism of the Indians towards unions, and the overall ignorance of the workers concerning grievance and collective bargaining procedures extend this litany of obstacles.

There is also a tradition of political apathy that is too often characteristic of the Latin American worker, especially the unorganized masses. Existing in poverty as his ancestors before him the ordinary person has had traditionally little interest in politics. Politics in any meaningful sense has been beyond his world, something for *los ricos.* In most Latin American countries only a very small percentage of the people actively participate in politics and can be said to represent an "informed" public opinion. While the picture varies in different countries, for the most part it reveals submerged masses of the virtually politically voiceless. To say this is not to forget that in recent decades, beginning particularly with the coming of the populist parties, there has been an increasing number of the poorer classes participating in electoral politics. But it must be remembered that politically as well as economically and socially the masses are decidedly limited. The relationship between labor and government throughout Latin America is fundamentally different from the western European, Canadian, or United States situation. In their development Latin American unions have had to depend much more upon government. While much assistance was given to trade unions they also became virtually captives of government. They are much more subject to interference by government in their internal affairs, and to use for political ends, than is the case in other western countries. As unionization developed governments promulgated labor legislation often with the purpose of helping labor but which, in effect, restricted labor's role. While it is true that workers are now protected by governmental action from arbitrary actions on the part of the employers, this results in the power of the state replacing the power of the manager. Labor, to repeat, is subject to governmental interferences not tolerated in advanced western countries.

In politics, therefore, while labor is an active participant and has made gains, its position in comparison with other interest groups is secondary. Politics for labor has too often meant gains for elite unions willing to collaborate with governments. And too often it has meant the use of a union or a confederation on the part of a labor leader to advance his own political future and his personal wealth.

All of these factors have contributed to making most of the organized working class a part of the conservative order. The majority of the important trade unions are, despite revolutionary slogans, run by leaders who have long since become a part of the system.[2]

On the positive side labor historically resembles a rising popular pressure group. In the twentieth century it came to challenge the power of those older organized corporate bodies, i.e., the landed oligarchs, the military, and the church, that have comprised the traditional ruling hierarchies, and their contemporary business successors.

The entrance of Latin America into the industrial age and the acceptance of trade unions as a mark of modernization has assisted those within the labor movement in their continuing struggle. Latin American labor leaders know that political parties and governments have shown an appreciation of the direct mass action that unions are capable of, the vehicle that labor affords for organizing supporters for political action in those countries where the influence of the ballot is important. Politicos in and out of government are aware of the militancy of labor and its weapon of the strike. They know the value of the strike when used as a political weapon. It is more frequently used in this manner than in the outside western countries because of Latin American labor's weakness as an organized political pressure group. Labor in Latin America has developed in several countries to the extent that it has some voice in the affairs of Centrist-to-Left political parties. There are members from the ranks of labor in many legislative bodies. Illustrations of labor's force in politics during the twentieth century are several and important. The decade following the Mexican revolution of 1910, the impact of labor upon Argentine politics beginning with the Peron dictatorship, the significance of labor in Chilean politics particularly in the *Unidad Popular* regime of Salvador Allende, are concrete examples. But for the most part labor is a subordinate partner among the various interest groups affecting Latin American politics.

The political history of Latin America for the most part is not one from which any democratic leader can draw much satisfaction and inspiration. The colonial rule of the European *peninsulares*, the many decades of authoritarianism when power was exercized after independence by the native *crillos*, the violence in the rule of *caudillo* and *junta militar* accepted or imposed as an alternative to chaos, the many superficial "palace" revolutions in contrast to the few genuine social upheavals—such is the main course of that history.

The twentieth century brought the three violent overturnings of the old social orders in the nationalistic Mexican revolution of 1910, and the Marxian-influenced Bolivian and Cuban upheavals at mid-century. The consequences of these revolutions, the development of populist nationalism with its appeals to the masses, and the later Christian humanistic socialistic appeals afford to such labor leaders as Jáuregui and Máspero in one way or other avenues to reaching the workers. Jáuregui has shown an interest in populism which continues. Máspero rejecting populism expresses a kind of extreme humanistic Christian radicalism. And whether it be the violent politics of Fidelist communism, the evolutionary approach advocated by most Latin American Communist leaders, or again the still different views of Marxists such as the Chilean Salvador Allende, each of our labor protagonists is vitally concerned with and affected by these radical expressions of contemporary politics.

Latin America's history of international relations and of foreign influences has mainly been concerned with the countries of western Europe and with the United States. The genesis of modern Latin America begins with the Spanish and Portuguese conquests of the native Indians. Like it or not the influence of the Iberian civilizations is indelibly stamped on the *latinos* and makes for particular continuing ties with Portugal and Spain. Spanish, along with Italian, ideological markings affected the history of Latin American labor, especially in the early anarchistic period. Italian and Spanish imprints are heavy in Argentina, Uruguay, and Chile. Modern Brazil exhibits the mixture of Italian, Portuguese, and African contributions. The cultural leadership of France has always been followed in a definite manner, particularly by the Latin American intellectual and upper classes. The commercial and other business interests of the Netherlands, Great Britain, and Germany especially, together with the military and naval models which the latter two nations furnished, are noteworthy in Latin American history.

In recent years, through foundations, quasi-governmental agencies, and similar types of corporate groups, representatives from foreign countries with a particular interest in labor activities have entered Latin America. The West German Ebert and Adenauer *Stifdungen*, and the American Institute for Free Labor Development of the United States are outstanding examples of this practice.

As is well known it is the United States, often called *el coloso del norte* by Latin Americans, that has come to be of major concern to our neighbors to the south. The Monroe doctrine, the Mexican War, the Spanish-American War are some of the obvious markings of the relationship. Since the turn of the century that relationship has been affected in innumerable ways—and from the Latin Americans point of view it has been one that has, in the net result, been adverse for them. In the post-World War II decades, particularly after the successful Castro revolution in Cuba, United States-Latin American relations have been affected by considerations of the cold war. Even before the coming of Castro to power the Soviet Union began to express for the first time an active interest in Latin American affairs. This interest has been reciprocated by Latin American nations and undoubtedly reflects their interest in demonstrating an independence from the United States. For whatever reasons the Soviet Union is now interested in Latin American affairs as never before.

The consequences of United States-Latin American relations and of Soviet-Latin American relations are of major concern to Jáuregui and Máspero. The United States as a capitalist country, the United States as a country with various business investments in Latin America, the touchy matter of U.S. intervention in the Southern Hemisphere, the Alliance for Progress, Pan Americanism, the cold war as it came to affect Latin America—these and other related matters affect the postures of the two rival labor leaders before Latin America and the world. More directly related to labor questions, the activities of the AFL-CIO in Latin American affairs—more or less closely related to the U.S. Department of

State—take on an increasing significance. Again, the new Soviet interest in Latin America, particularly with its help to Cuba and with regard to Communist strategy and tactics with regard to trade unions, are of particular interest.

Such then is the historical and contemporary "setting" in which the rivalry between ORIT and CLAT (recently evolved from CLASC) must be seen. The examination of some of the factors, particularly the U.S.-Soviet tensions as they affected Latin America and bore upon the policies of the leaders considered here constitutes a major part of this study. At this juncture we may observe in general fashion their respective attitudes toward the United States and the Soviet Union.

Jáuregui, as might be expected, is almost consistently friendly both to the U.S. government and to his brother North American trade unionists regarding activities affecting Latin America. Máspero, in a word, is almost consistently critical. At the same time Jáuregui is emphatic that he and his fellow *latinos* are "no colonials" of the United States. At times he will criticize the U.S. government and actions within the AFL-CIO power elite. Máspero, the overall critic of the United States, periodically distinguishes between the American governments of recent decades, the majority of the American labor leaders, and the American people as a whole, and several important American labor leaders whom he admires.

Concerning Moscow and its activities in Latin America each labor leader is critical. But Jáuregui has been critical virtually without qualifications. He is convinced that the Communist powers and communism in Latin America in one fashion or other constitute a threat that must always be taken seriously. The strategy and tactics of the Soviet Union may change, along with that of the Communists in Latin America, it may at times be at odds with that of some of the Communist leaders in Latin America, but it remains a threat that cannot ever be taken lightly. It would require a miracle to bring about any attitude of cooperation in Latin America between Jáuregui and Communists of any persuasion. While the occasional critic of *el coloso del norte*, Jáuregui is a friend of the United States. He is the continuing critic of Soviet and Communist imperialism in any shape or form.

Máspero, while critical of Soviet imperialism and of Soviet actions concerning trade unionism in Latin America, and fundamentally opposed to communism, believes that United States imperialism is a greater danger to Latin America than that of the Soviet Union. For strategic purposes Máspero on occasion would cooperate with Latin American Communists to achieve certain common ends. But his suspicion of American government, business, and AFL-CIO labor leaders and their policies appears even deeper and more abiding than his fundamentally negative view of communism and critical attitude toward the Soviet Union. To repeat, to him, the Soviet Union is a newcomer into the southern Western Hemisphere. Its imperialistic interests are evident, but they are more forcefully expressed elsewhere. It is *el coloso del norte*'s imperialism that represents the greater danger. History and contemporary affairs tell Máspero this.[3]

3 Conflicting Perspectives I: Ideology

In light of the circumstances resulting from the particular Latin American "setting," what are the means that each aspiring leader uses to achieve his goals? What are the factors—such as the resources commanded, the values each assumes, the interpretations of the possibilities to achieve the goals in view of the nature of the social *ambiente*—that influence the kind of direction each gives and which have shaped their organizations into what they have become under their leaders? How important have Jáuregui and Máspero regarded the need for their respective labor groups to be motivated by an ideology? What has been the nature of the ideological expression during their tenures?

A consideration of these questions demonstrates that these professedly democratic labor leaders, each an advocate of the need for a social revolution, are fundamentally in conflict.

Máspero and Jáuregui know that in the stratified hierarchical Latin American society trade unions have been regarded as a revolutionary force. They are fully aware that labor in its origins was viewed as in some manner an agency of those demanding changes in the restricted political, economic, and social institutions, changes which would benefit the underprivileged masses. They know that in the Latin American ambient the very effort to organize the unorganized was (and still is in some areas) regarded as essentially a revolutionary act.

As representatives of the newest political corporate group, spokesmen for organized labor sought to enter the centers of power in order to gain for themselves and their supporters a fuller share of the gross production and public services. Such action demonstrated the potential of organized labor to assume the role of representatives of the long excluded and exploited masses. Whether or not they come to realize this potential the leaders of organized labor have challenged the power of the traditional corporate groups—the landed and industrial oligarchs, the Church, and the military. In this challenge, and even more in its apparent efforts to speak and to act for the underdogs of Latin America, trade unionism reveals at least its potential, if not actual, revolutionary thrust. It is generally true that trade unionism became an agency of conformity. But with a new inspiration it might assist in the change which in one form or other is present, or struggles for birth, throughout Latin America. Jáuregui and Máspero avow that they are directing their organizations along the social revolutionary route.

Agreed on the necessity of basic social change, the rival hemispheric labor leaders have different views as to its nature and the way in which it will be attained; while in many cases they appear to use the same kinds of facilities, they also employ distinctly different ways and means to achieve their goals. Summarily stated, Jáuregui speaks of social revolution in less radical democratic terms and pursues a more pragmatic and less militant strategy and tactics than does the CLAT leader. Jáuregui, broadly speaking, seeks to advance labor's interest by working within the system and by supporting an extension of the democratic populist politics. While the actual type of economic order sought will vary in different countries, he broadly envisions a revised efficient "mixed economy" developed through the positive state. In moving towards the progressive new order he believes in accepting North American assistance to improve union conditions and the standard of living of the individual worker.

Máspero makes a more direct frontal attack against capitalism and the present social institutions and insists that the task of the revolution must be accomplished by Latin American workers themselves. Jáuregui believes that the use of governmental or private technical aid is important in what he regards as a revolutionary process while Máspero is either outrightly suspicious of such aid or views it as negligible in aiding the necessary fundamental change.

Jáuregui's Stance

The nature of the rival labor confederations—such factors as size, resources, the prestige of the affiliated unions, and the values that these affiliates emphasize— are significant in helping to shape the views that each leader has of himself and his major goals. Due to the inter-American character of the ORIT, Jáuregui numbers experienced North American trade unionists among his supporters. With a Latin American membership of important older unions the ORIT leader also enjoys closer relations with more Latin American governments and political parties. He also has, to say the least, far better contacts at U.S. embassies.

Using these resources Jáuregui has pursued his efforts at improving the workers' conditions, mainly by the more familiar means of pressures applied by affiliates, and the election of members of political parties pledged to alter the status quo through democratic processes. The long-range job of developing greater maturity in unions by stressing the importance of workers' education both narrowly and broadly conceived, the expanding of educational facilities and programs, the extension of collective bargaining (which among other aspects he believes strongly aids in building a sense of workers' solidarity), the increase of labor research activities—all these under Jáuregui have become even more than previously the marks of the ORIT's stance. In the matter of workers' education and social development, as well as in other less formalized training, Jáuregui has welcomed whatever assistance the AFL-CIO or American embassies have provided over the years. The charges from his critics, of course, are that the ORIT has become a façade for the AFL-CIO and the U.S. Department of State. Despite these charges, and the personal irritations that have developed periodically from the nature of what he regards as a necessary relationship with American trade union leaders and their representatives within the ORIT complex, Jáuregui believes that he has managed to maintain American support without sacrificing his *dignidad*—or, he asserts, that of the Latin American members of the ORIT.

Secretary general of an organization whose genesis was partly the desire to construct a bulwark against the spread of communism, Jáuregui's opposition to communism in any of the varieties in which it expresses itself has been more marked than any of the previous occupants of the office in ORIT history. The development of matured democratic unionism which is his ultimate goal, he believes, requires this constant vigilance against communism. He also avowedly stands against fascism and dictatorship in any form. What Jáuregui sees as the CLAT's dividing tactics during years when, according to him, the weak Latin American labor movement was (and is) beset with threats from communism and other undemocratic forces, is a particular reason for his antipathy to the rival Christian grouping.

A frequent hemispheric and world traveler, Jáuregui has borne the ORIT message to such agencies as the Alliance for Progress, the Organization of American States, as well as to global labor forums provided by the International Confederation of Free Trade Unions and the International Labor Office. And as an avid believer in short courses and forums for educating Latin American workers, he has arranged for the presence of officials of national and international reputation from various hemispheric and global agencies, both from the world of labor government and education, to participate in the programs which are a part of the broad educational activities of the ORIT's hemispheric education center in Cuernavaca, Mexico.

The nature of the ORIT being what it is, Jáuregui has to face the various continuing problems that arise from the character of its affiliates. Concerning his relations with the more powerful of the Latin American affiliates his critics assert that he is too friendly to the *latino* union bureaucrats, to those who despite noble utterances concerning their devotion to the union rank and file are more interested in furthering their own interests as members of political parties in control of governments to which, at bottom, labor is a captive. For example, the accusation has been made that ORIT exists in its Mexico City headquarters only as long as the predominant Mexican labor body, the powerful CTM, the long-time favorite labor confederation of the ruling political party of Mexico (the PRI), is satisfied with the policies of the ORIT.[a] It is further asserted that the ORIT has other affiliates in which a bureaucratization dominating the ordinary members in the interests of the top leadership is characteristic.

---

[a]After many years occupying offices in downtown Mexico City at the Plaza de la Republica owned by a CTM affiliate, ORIT transferred its headquarters to a large private home in the southern part of the city in the fall of 1972. Some critics say that this was due to unfriendly pressure by the CTM officialdom. Jáuregui labels the charge as "ridiculous and petty."

So to the familiar charge that Jáuregui is a captive of the Yankee union gold is added the accusation that he is also controlled by self-serving, dishonest native labor *caudillos* in league with political or economic interests that are detrimental to the ordinary worker. Such conditions, say his critics, make a mockery of the efforts to promote democratic trade unionism throughout the hemisphere.

Confronted with such attacks the ORIT secretary general reacts, to quote him, as a "pragmatic realist." He believes in the politics of compromise to achieve his goals. He insists that whatever negligible degree of validity may exist in the charges, it is canceled by the achievements of the ORIT which have been made under the most trying conditions. He asserts that all the circumstances in the Latin American setting—in the society and political area—must be fully accounted for when one passes judgment. This means remembering that he leads a regional organization of completely autonomous national confederations which operate in a Latin America of varying degrees of poverty, ignorance, and misery, and of varying degrees of rigid social stratification, where deference has traditionally given to the powerful personalist figure, and where trade unions have generally had to accept government assistance and controls as the price of their development. In view of these facts Jáuregui believes that what he and others in the ORIT have brought about is in truth a miracle. That miracle he feels is mainly compounded of the progress that has been made in keeping the Latin American labor movement out of Communist control into which it was slipping before the ORIT was organized, of the progress made in the difficult task of building and developing truly democratic trade unions, and the success in using the union pressure to advance the social welfare of the people.

To specific CLAT charges concerning Jáuregui's and ORIT's compromising relations with Fidel Velasquez, powerful long-time leader of the Workers' Confederacion of Mexico (CTM), Jáuregui replies that the ORIT is fortunate to have a warm supporter in the CTM leader whom he, Jáuregui, is glad to acknowledge as a friend. He reminds his critics, however, that in its early history, when the CTM led by Fidel Valesquez withdrew from ORIT, that regional organization continued unhampered on its course of development. It was a highly satisfactory matter to Jáuregui personally and other leaders in ORIT, that Velasquez on his own initiative accepted the invitation of ORIT to rejoin that body on 1953, although at this time ORIT did not give way to Señor Velasquez's urging that it admit the Argentinian CGT. (This was the matter that had caused CTM's withdrawal from ORIT's founding convention in 1951.)

As to CLAT's most recent charges that Señor Velasquez is unhappy with Jáuregui and ORIT, Jáuregui dismisses them as continued attempts to try to divide and weaken ORIT. He mentions his continued friendship with Velasquez and the past criticisms that his rivals have made of the CTM leader as a labor boss at the service of the PRI. Jáuregui has always taken the position that Fidel Velasquez has ably represented the interests of Mexican workers before the PRI.

Jáuregui dwells upon the accomplishments represented in the training of promising young workers not only in the important more narrowly related skills but in the techniques of democratic decision-making. The youth, the hope of the future, live in an area of the hemisphere not particularly accustomed to the virtues of democratic practices. These youthful products of workers' education in the broadest sense, he believes, will be operationalizing their ORIT schooling, gradually changing the less pleasant features in the labor picture as it exists today.

It is, therefore, worth underscoring that during his tenure Jáuregui has stressed the educational function of the ORIT. The ORIT school in Cuernavaca, built in 1966, was primarily the result of Jáuregui's vision and tireless devotion. The training of the ORIT's most promising young *latino* trade unionists takes place in the Cuernavaca center. Jáuregui's devotion to developing workers' education in a broad sense is also reflected in the special programs periodically held in Cuernavaca. It is further expressed in the conferences that he has helped to arrange (and generally has participated in as a spokesman) throughout the hemisphere and periodically throughout the western world. In recent years both in union schools and in special conferences Jáuregui has been underscoring the importance of women in industry and of the long neglected workers, the *campesinos*, to the organized labor movement.[1] He has directed the attention of Latin American labor leaders to various programs for cooperation between the different countries in order to encourage the process of economic integration which has concerned Latin Americans for many years. In all of these more recent interests he has, as from the beginning, welcomed the cooperation of North American trade unionists.

Jáuregui's view of what constitutes the social revolution and of labor's role in sustaining and nourishing it is what he believes is, to repeat him, "the pragmatic long view." Agreed that specific strategies and tactics will vary in different countries, his overall belief is that the revolutionary force labor represents should be used in a democratic fashion to bring about necessary basic social, political, and economic changes. He believes that nationalism, industrial development, social welfare, and change in social status—in other words, the components of social revolution—must be nourished. Doing this will take time, for the social revolution must rest on firm foundations. The achievement of the revolution is seen as the consequence of a step-by-step process. Such a process, working within the system, engaging in practical politics, and compromising when necessary, is admittedly often frustrating. According to Jáuregui, however, the ORIT does not make compromises that in the long run sacrifice the essential autonomy and independence of the labor movements. Within the labor movement itself, he argues, all that helps labor to grow to maturity aids towards its participation in the shaping of social revolution. Thus, the great need for developing formal and informal workers' education, the learning techniques of organization, of morale building, and of collective bargaining. Thus, the need to accept the aid of North American workers where these experienced brother workers can assist through advice and aid to strengthen the democratic development in Latin American organized labor. Thus, the need to combat any efforts at penetration of the Latin American labor movement by dictatorial or totalitarin forces. And thus, too, Jáuregui would insist, the need to resist *all* imperialisms.

Jáuregui believes that due to the ORIT's more practical nonflamboyant approach his critics have disregarded its solid accomplishments as a careful builder of and contributer to necessary progressive social change. His answer to those who say that ORIT's ideology and practice have been timid, cautious, and too pragmatic (and consequently that it fails to really advance a social revolution) is a blunt rejection of the charges. "We do not have to pay attention to the words of our enemies. We are in favor of social revolution but we just don't talk about it from balconies. We are helping in practice to make it."[2]

In comparison to Máspero, who from the beginning of his leadership of the CLASC revealed a fervent interest in constructing a distinctive belief system for the organization Jáuregui, until recently, was not overly concerned with the importance of ideology. His attitude to some degree reflected the position of the bulk of ORIT's membership—the important older, city-oriented (for the most part) Latin American unions, and the powerful North Americans. The Latin American members for the most part come from national confederations of unions established between the First and Second World Wars, or shortly after the Second World War when interest in immediate political tactics superseded the earlier union interest in ideology. The AFL-CIO experience reflects a successful history of pragmatic "bread-and-butter" non-class conflict trade unionism.

Prior to 1970 when the ORIT, largely through Jáuregui's prodding, began to give serious attention to the importance of ideology the ORIT's principle formal expression of its beliefs was found in "The Philosophy of ORIT: A Statement of the Principles of the Free Inter-American Labor Movement," first published in the summer of 1963. This statement is, according to a recent statement of Jáuregui, ORIT's ideology "in the past, present, and future" which does not, he adds, mean that it cannot be improved upon.

At the outset "The Philosophy" asserts its belief in the unity of the workers of all the Americas, a unity seen as necessary for overcoming various obstacles including those of primitive conditions, underdevelopment, language, and geography. It is repeatedly asserted that "within the framework of the new trade unionism, which is democratic and revolutionary in content," the ICFTU and the ORIT have sought to put into practice the motto "Bread, Peace, Freedom." Economic democracy must, it states, be combined with political democracy if social justice for the workers is to be achieved. The ORIT "has consistently maintained there can be no economic development or social progress without the direct participation of democratically organized workers in study, planning and execution of projects for economic and social development." All forms of totalitarianism are attacked, with Fidel Castro's regime in Cuba being specifically cited. A warning is given concerning "the ominous influence of militarism in Latin America."

In the struggle for the extension of democracy and social justice the manifesto underscores the need for raising the levels of knowledge of trade union leaders in the less developed countries. Supporting freedom, it flatly rejects colonialism and imperialism. In its fight against economic imperialism the document states that the "ORIT has the valuable suport of the strongest trade union organizations of the United States which have identified themselves with the Latin American peoples in their struggles." The Alliance for Progress, which had recently come into being, is specifically endorsed.

Such, in summary fashion, was for years the formal ideological statement of the ORIT. It can be fairly classified as a pragmatic, common-sense doctrine of inter-American cooperation in the struggle to achieve social justice and democracy. While it asserts a belief in social revolution there is no discussion in depth of what constitutes the revolution and how it is to be made. Nor is there any spelling out of the particular kind of economic order that the "economic democracy" it seeks entails. It represents a very general and eclectic type of statement.

In recent years Jáuregui has sought to direct the ORIT toward the consideration of the significance of ideology. Largely due to his efforts considerable attention was given to the importance of a sociopolitical program during the Twentieth Anniversary Conference in Mexico City and Cuernavaca, Mexico, in January 1971. In the various sessions a newer, more militant tone was revealed by some of the speakers. An examination of the meaning of democracy at great length exhibited this feeling. The influence of the United States and the Soviet Union upon smaller nations in obliging them to ascribe to the official ideologies sponsored by these superpowers was criticized. The problem of the obstacles to forming an authentic ideology that the native oligarchies' support of foreign colonialism constitutes also was examined.

Some of the participants frankly criticized "international capitalism" and defended a type of democratic socialism. The need to construct and extend ideological appeals to the *campesinos* was underscored. It was recommended that increased emphasis be put upon understanding ideologies in the curricula of workers education in the ORIT Institute in Cuernavaca. In connection with the work of the ORIT Labor College (the Cuernavaca Institute) increased attention to organizing *campesino* programs and seminars was advised.

The militant democratic radicalism that was expressed by some of the delegates warrants quotation. Thus, Julio Cruzado, secretary general of the CTP, of Peru, said in part: "The old ideologies which yesterday served the superpowers (i.e., the United States and the Soviet Union) as a justification for their national behavior have continued to play a star role in the underdeveloped regions of the world and especially Latin America."[3] And again:

(The) attitude of the Latin American leaders would seem to be based on the supposition that social change in Latin America shall be brought to us from on high, be it through those financial and technical assistance programs that are designed with generous motives but with a total ignorance of our realities, or through the tactics of struggle adapted to the world strategy of a dominant power and not to the needs of underdeveloped countries that can and must apply methods of liberation which are original and which have no ties to foreign interests.[4]

Solferino Ferreti and Lina Cortizo of the CUT, of Uruguay, while strongly critical of communism, "a system to be implanted in our countries, a system that has weakened trade union action," coupled this with attacks on "the economic and political groups committed to capitalism," on large corporations, and on the regimes in Latin America which hypocritically use free election to advance the interests of the oligarchies at the expense of the workers.[5]

Several of the most militant statements came from *campesino* spokesmen, Arturo Morales Cubas, leader of the Federated Workers Union of Guatemala, and Armando Gonzales, president of the Peasant Federation of Venezuela (CTV). Morales Cubas raised the following question:

... How are you going to blame a peasant who chooses the path of violence when he is unprotected by the laws, when his family is dying of hunger or tuberculosis, when there is illiteracy, subhuman housing, when there is contempt and neglect, and where there are bullets to restrain those who want to rise up and really demand a right that as humans living in the twentieth century they are entitled to? [6]

His federation, he said, asked "that discussion be set aside and that we determine what the fight in all of America, but especially in Latin America, really requires." ORIT's role, he continued is "difficult, but beautiful, if it knows how to fulfill its obligation. Otherwise, we shall not be able to believe in speeches."[7]

Armando Gonzales played a most prominent part in the conference. His observations ranged over many topics—the need for a new action—oriented system of ideas, the necessity to revive the clearer sense of international solidarity possessed by the workers of the previous century, the problems presented by the challenges of the then CLASC and the Communists, the intensification of propaganda among the *campesino* and worker masses to use those political parties that can be made instruments of social and economic struggle, and the continuing and gigantic problem presented by capitalism which through great corporations and great consortiums produces dehumanized societies. Throughout, the Venezuelan *campesino* leader's expositions references to "the proletariat and its organizations," the strengthening of "class solidarity," and the "organized force of workers" as the instrument to balance "those who possess the means of production" were made. The ORIT was called upon to construct a doctrine "ideologically free of servility" by means of which it "can be the coherent factor required by the masses of Latin America to put an end to the degrading and feudalistic latifundism that exists there."[8]

In concluding his remarks at the session summarizing the discussions of the conference, Señor Gonzales dwelt on the relation of the ORIT to social revolution, and the need for an ideology that would attract the masses and prevent them from being wooed by the promises of the new advanced right (including the CLASC), or by the Communist world.

A revolution constitutes the supreme instrument to which the masses can resort at a given moment thoroughly to transform that which exists: economic, juridical, social and even cultural structures. That is why, if the Latin American masses should be in need of resorting to this instrument in one, many, or all countries, the ORIT ought to be in a position to channel, orientate and direct this revolutionary movement toward the free world's objectives.[9]

And with reference to the possibility of the masses being beguiled by the promises of the advanced right and the Communists, he said:

Therefore, in order that this may not occur, it is urgent that we, the free trade union movement of Latin America, be in the capacity to create the organizational structure—with a clear ideology, with philosophic principles and a theory and strategy—needed to make possible a victorious confrontation with any of the other ideologies currently endeavoring to dominate the world.[10]

It is clear that in the consideration of ideology at the conference, (a matter which was largely the result of Jáuregui's planning), a radical overtone and a deeper investigation of the importance of the concept than in all the previous years of the ORIT's existence was in evidence. What this portends for the future only time will make clear. In his closing remarks Jáuregui, in accepting all comments and criticisms in a positive fashion, pointed out that the ORIT while handicapped financially has been strengthened in its trade union mysticism to overcome many problems. The ORIT, he said, being a democratic organization and composed of autonomous bodies from different countries has an arduous path to travel in arriving at an ideology and political action acceptable to the whole organization. He noted that some of the confederations in Latin America were "ashamed, or afraid of publishing ORIT statements for fear of communism, or of the Social-Christian forces, or the national forces, or the governments in turn." He also asserted that in the ORIT Labor College "merely craft or trade unionism, strictly speaking, is not taught here but trade unionism with much ideological content."[11]

While Jáuregui has demonstrated a new interest in ideology he remains a pragmatist. He contrasts the practical accomplishments of ORIT with the "talk" of the CLASC (turned CLAT) in its numerous "quickie" seminars which he sees as its principle activity. To Jáuregui the smaller rival organization appears as a group of missionaries working principally in the interest of certain church, labor, and governmental interests located outside Latin America. These people he believes have intruded into the hemisphere to obstruct and divide a Latin American labor movement that is admittedly weak. CLAT, to him, is a reckless body interfering with the ORIT's efforts to develop democratic trade unionism and to fight against totalitarianism.

To Jáuregui CLAT, like CLASC before it, is not a legitimate labor body. Its actual, really viable trade union strength, he insists, is negligible. He reiterates that the strongest unions of Catholic inspiration in Latin America, the *Union de Trabajadores de Colombia* and the Costa Rican *Costaricense de Trabajo* are affiliated with the ORIT. The vast majority of the affiliates of the CLAT he insists are weak groupings or unions that really have little more existence than their names on the organizations' letterheads. CLAT operates organizationally mainly as a group of unionists affiliated to it as individuals. That, he avers, is the so-called regional labor organization that arrogantly calls upon Latin American labor to disavow the democratic, larger, viable ORIT, and unite to build a purely Latin American democratic confederation.

In Emilio Máspero, from Jáuregui's perspective, the European clerical and secular motivators of the CLASC (now CLAT), who are also the major sources of its financial strength, have discovered a brash, youthful, loquacious, "ex-seminarian" with little actual experience as a worker at the shop level, but an admittedly gifted orator and manipulating politician—a *caudillo*—to lead their Latin American intrusion. Máspero's brashness and assertiveness may, it is true, cause some of the European elite embarrassment but, says Jáuregui, they know that he is the best man in Latin America for carrying out their particular job of attempting to obstruct the ORIT in the interests of European governmental and confessional groups.

As Jáuregui sees it Máspero has "talked revolution" while accomplishing little or nothing of a practical nature that contributes concretely to the actual making of basic social change. Romantic orations about the revolution, the aggressive posture of Máspero and his organization, and the extreme anti-Americanism, do not, says Jáuregui, in the end bring positive gains to labor.

While the ORIT leader periodically seeks to belittle positive accomplishments of Máspero and the CLAT, he does underscore his rival's divisive potential. To Jáuregui, Máspero has viciously exploited one of the oldest demagogic tricks in Latin America—Yankee-baiting. Drawing upon that easily available weapon, Máspero he believes has unfairly criticized the United States policies, and the friendly effort of trade unionists in the United States, which are aimed at alleviating misery in Latin America and strengthening Latin American trade unionism. Máspero has linked the AFL-CIO activity inside the ORIT and the AIFLD as part of American imperialism in Latin America. He has pictured the American trade unionists as the paid agents of their government. He has declared the ORIT itself as an instrument of Yankee imperialism. Máspero, according to Jáuregui, has done all this fully aware of the damage that such charges could accomplish to labor unity in Latin America.

At the same time Jáuregui charges that Máspero has in practice largely soft-pedaled his criticisms of Russia and communism while periodically he has worked with the Communists on common objectives. Máspero's extreme attack upon capitalism together with his frequent call to revolution are a further illustration of the demagogue and contribute to the eventual damaging possibility—the division of the Latin American labor movement. A further weakening of labors' forces by Máspero, according to this perspective, is his "confessionalism" by means of which the CLAT leader is seeking to replace the secular nature of free democratic trade unionism with a labor ideology that in inspiration is clerical and Christian Democrat. "Máspero," Jáuregui has declared, "is above all a political militant who works for the Christian Democratic movement and is financially supported with the aid of the German bishops."[12]

Such in brief compass is the character of Máspero and his organization as Jáuregui sees them. Máspero may talk of social revolution and of the role of labor in making that revolution. In reality he is a romantic (if brilliant) demagogue seeking to advance himself as he postures before Latin America, using the support of European backers to seek to achieve his ends. Romanticizing about social revolution, including the possibility of having to use violence to achieve it, Máspero really contributes little in the long difficult task of making a truly democratic revolution. It bears repeating that what Jáuregui does feel is that Máspero might succeed in dividing and disrupting the democratic elements in Latin American labor which have worked so long at the task of advancing a practical genuine social revolution—one that the ORIT leader says is measured by achievements and not by rhetoric. To Jáuregui it is fantastic that the CLASC (or CLAT) should criticize the ORIT's attack on communism, its use of American trade union aid to fight communism, or its alliance with the AIFLD in a positive program of educational organizational and technical accomplishments which limit communism's appeal. These criticisms are all the more galling from the ORIT leader's viewpoint when it is remembered that Máspero and company have at times for their own tactical reasons joined with Communists in a common action program. Máspero and his people, from the Jáuregui perspective, have also played into the Communist hands by attacking parties of the democratic left that the ORIT supports, such as Peru's *Apristas*, Costa Rica's *Liberación Nacional*, and Venezuela's *Acción Democrática*. Whatever his own differences with the powerful Yankee trade unionists, the ORIT leader has little patience with Máspero's views on this matter. He denies that the AFL-CIO dominates the ORIT by virtue of its wealth and asserts that the AFL-CIO's financial and technical assistance is for programs that seek to alleviate widespread misery among Latin American workers. To him the ORIT, with its North American and Latin American components, its sister organization the AIFLD, and whatever U.S. governmental or private individuals who in one way or other help these organizations, are, at bottom, assisting in forwarding social progress in Latin America. Whatever criticisms he himself makes of the ORIT's relations with its American supporters, Jáuregui insists that out of the relationship have emerged solid "practical revolutionary" achievements.[b]

For Jáuregui it is essential to repeat that social justice, the heart of the revolution, must be obtained through a democratic politics that underlines the importance of national independence and stable government. This, given the Latin American history and ambiente is a truly difficult task. "It is also at times difficult to work with the powerful Yankees when you are poor." The ORIT leader knows all this but he asserts that he welcomes the challenge.

Jáuregui in sum strives to bring about what he considers social revolution by working in all ways which he believes are best suited to the realities of the various Latin American nations. He deplores any attempt or consideration of violent revolution and reiterates time and again that he stands against all varients of Communist as well as non-Communist totalitarianism. His faith is in a peaceful revolution achieved by democratic means. This fundamental change will take time and will be achieved mainly by hard work within the system. The ORIT standard according to Jáuregui is "revolution, renovation, confrontation, reforms."[13] His revolution, however, is not of the sweeping variety. If it is a revolution sought through renovation, confrontation and reforms it is conducted by evolutionary means. It insists on change—but without great disturbance if possible.

Máspero's Stance

Emilio Máspero, personally and operationally, in his politics is more militant than his rival. Considerably smaller in size than the ORIT, with few well-established trade union affiliates, but with a greater attraction for the newer more revolutionary peasant groupings, the CLASC under his leadership acted primarily as a "labor missionary" force for social revolution. It was secondarily (if importantly) a confederation for organizing and building trade unions. Many workers joined the CLASC as individual unionists, although the regional body had labor unions as well as its affiliates. From its origin the CLASC had sought to be a third force between Communist-controlled unions and the ORIT, and true to its mission it had also been willing to cooperate with any "free" union to try to develop a united labor front of Latin American labor in the cause of a people's social revolution.

Máspero, a gifted orator and tireless worker, like Jáuregui has been concerned with such practical matters as workers' education, the female worker, and the

---

[b]Specific illustrations of Jáuregui's various disagreements with the AFL-CIO are discussed below.

extension of trade unionism to the countryside.[14] He, too, like Jáuregui, uses various seminars and congresses and periodic appearances at hemispheric and international governmental and private bodies concerned with labor to press his case as widely as possible. Support of political parties is also followed. But his overall tactics and message are decidedly different from those of his rival. As the leader of the younger, smaller, but more militant organization he does not enjoy as much contact through formal channels with the majority of the Latin American governments and politicians as does Jáuregui. His workers' education programs are, like those of the ORIT, concerned with matters of practical interest to the workers, but from the beginning they were, in addition, much more directed to building a mystique for making revolution. In a word, particularly since the coming of Máspero's regime, the underlying concern of the CLASC (which continues in the CLAT) is the social revolution. "Revolution, renovation, confrontation, reform"—Jáuregui's standard for the ORIT could be also that of Máspero and the CLASC. With the latter leader, however, the operationalization reveals no inclination to moderation in the efforts aimed at changing an intolerable social order.

Máspero came to the CLASC bearing the imprint of the left-wing Christian Democrat. Ever since his own regime within the CLASC began in 1966 he has increasingly stressed the need for radical measures. Both at home and in the important European councils he has carried the militant torch. Despite misgivings of some European Christians and their supporters (as well as some Latin Americans), Máspero from the beginning in his call for revolution has emphasized an anti-United States, anti-imperialist, anti-capitalist, anti-Soviet, pro-socialist line.

The transformation of the CLASC into the CLAT (the Latin American Worker's Central) during the Sixth Congress of the CLASC held in Caracas at the end of November 1971, marked the further extension of Máspero's democratic radicalism. Reasserted at this meeting were the militant revolutionary themes that had increasingly characterized the CLASC during Máspero's leadership—the attacks on capitalism and its institutions, opposition to North American and Soviet imperialism in Latin America, the identification of his organization with the peoples of the Third World, the pledge to fight for a new pluralistic society of the workers firmly committed to democracy. In great detail the Congress spelled out the strategy and politics which must be followed by the CLAT. These include emphasis upon a non-Marxian doctrine of intensified class conflict, appeals to workers in Latin America associated with organizations of the North American and Soviet enemy, as well as to the workers of the mother countries in those imperialist nations, and an analysis of imperialism together with suggestions for how it should be combatted. Attention was also directed to the social conflicts that were seen as becoming daily more evident within the United States and the Soviet Union.

The change in name from Latin American Christian Trade Unions to the

Latin American Workers Central (from CLASC to CLAT), and the critical examination of the problem of clericalism, declared to be one of the most persistant forms of paternalism within Latin America, underscored the desire to eliminate any doubts concerning this radical Christian-inspired labor grouping's freedom from Church influence. Crucially related to the transformation of the CLASC to the CLAT is the desire to proclaim the organization as being more than a trade union movement. It is no longer a hemispheric confederation of just *unionists* or *unions*, but a *central*, a *workers'* movement in the broadest sense of the term. It seeks to enlist all types of workers in overthrowing the present system and building a workers' democracy. The Congress thus issued a special appeal to nonunion professional people.

Some of the other concerns examined were the universities and students in relation to the workers, the sensitive issue of birth control and the different avenues of affinity of Latin American workers to the activities of workers throughout the Third World. Repeatedly the theme of the workers' struggle was underlined with the admonition that in the class struggle the workers must rely on themselves to emancipate themselves. "Only the people can save the people" was the slogan.

Emilio Máspero played a leading role in this Congress as one of the founding fathers of the CLAT. And he continued his militancy revolutionary secular exposition in the more exclusively ideological statement "El Papel De Los Trabajadores En La Construccion Del Socialismo Comunitario" ("The Role of the Workers in the Construction of Communitarian Socialism"), presented to a conference in Merida, Venezuela, in July 1972. All the evidence points in the direction indicating that in his latest expositions, as in his earlier ones, Máspero is supported by the elite of various European Christian-inspired groups and the World Confederation of Labor.[15]

Historically Latin America has been dominated by the landed and industrial oligarchs and their associates of the church and military in the interests of the wealthy. This bad situation Máspero feels, continues, with the privileged now occasionally using the farcical technique of legal political democracy to continue to sustain their position.

Unlike Jáuregui, Máspero does not believe that there is much to be achieved from supporting the popular "*Aprista*-type" parties, or perhaps better stated, that much can today be expected of these parties—the PRI of Mexico, *Accion Democratica* of Venezuela, *Liberacion* of Costa Rica, and the APRA itself in contemporary Peru. Populist parties, he says, in effect, at one time did give promise of being instrumentalities of fundamental change, but they have long since become respectable supporters of the status quo. No matter what improvements they have made they are no longer revolutionary parties. At best they are reformist, at worst they serve the interests of the rich and the middle class.

Emphatically a nationalist, who believes that foreign models are not to be imitated, Máspero sees no positive advantage accruing to labor from the AFL-CIO examples. North American trade unions developed in a country with a different history from that which is Latin America's. Collective bargaining, pragmatic evolutionary techniques which soften social divisions between owners or managers and workers may be good for North American trade unions. Latin America, however, is an area in which intense class conflicts and ideologies have a long history. The conditions there are such that this militancy must continue. Thus North American labor models are not for Latin Americans.

During the years of the CLASC Máspero stood with the radical, anti-capitalist elements in the Latin American Christian Democracy in a radical humanistic socialist direction. His claims of CLASC strength in helping to achieve the Chilean Christian Democratic victory in 1964 is supposed to have annoyed the more centrist elements of that party. Máspero, however, has not confined his admiration exclusively to left-wing Christians. In recent years he has spoken favorably of the democratically-elected-Marxist Allende regime in Chile. He supports all movements that in his opinion help the workers.

To seek to capture power—democratically where that is possible—to end the old intolerable order in the interest of the dispossessed and to build a worker's democracy always was the goal avowed by Máspero. This was the impression I had in the conversations I had with him, in Santiago in the fall of 1966. His writings, speeches and activities since have underscored his missionary role. The CLASC and now the CLAT under Máspero has continuously expounded an ideology. This concern reveals Máspero's conviction of the necessity of arming the worker with an explanation of their sorry lot, a means of self-identification, a guide to conduct, a promise of a new and better life—in a word of giving to the workers an ideology.

From the beginning of his regime the CLASC message was a strong humanistic message—asserting the importance of the individual worker, the need of the workers to join with their fellows to construct a brotherhood of self-respecting individuals. The people, it said, must come to the realization that they are the source of true power. While government is necessary, and technology is necessary, the people are primary. It is the people who must unite and put government and technology to work for the common good. The message in one fashion or other has been an underlying theme with the CLASC from Máspero's early days.[c]

In the dogma that only Latin Americans should belong to their revolutionary workers' movement Máspero made the special appeal to the members to have pride in themselves as ordinary men and women, and as Latin Americans. For if they do not have such pride and belief that they can accomplish, that they are the source of a great potential power, then the native *oligarquia* and their

---

[c]I have been told many times by both critics and friends of the CLASC that the Jesuit Roger Vekemans, Máspero's early sponsor when he sought refuge in Chile, is also responsible for this ideology. Vekemans and Máspero parted company several years ago.

associates the foreign interventionists, particularly in the United States, will continue to control. In this underscoring of the importance of people, there is again a reminder to government that its being rests upon the people's will.

This radical message, begun in the early days of the Máspero's leadership, has always been incorporated into the resolutions of larger gatherings of workers that came together under CLASC sponsorship. For as indicated the CLASC, while it saw itself as the trade union third force in Latin America between the Communists and the capitalists, always strongly indicated its interest in joining with all labor elements which can be united in a common front against common enemies. The same theme has been repeated in the transformation to the CLAT, in which the CLASC's earlier message has been expanded under Máspero into a stronger ideological statement.

Ideology – The CLASC

One of the best examples of such CLASC sponsored general workers' meetings in which the radical democratic people's ideology was expounded, was the so-called "First Trade Union Conference on Latin American Development and Integration" held in Santo Domingo May 20-24, 1968. Máspero was one of the chief organizers of this conference. The Dominican Republic is the locale of one of the few significant trade union groups affiliating with the CLASC (now CLAT) the *Confederación Autonoma de Sindicatos Christianós* (CASC). Through CASC the CLASC enjoyed a strength within the Dominican Republic's labor movement that has successfully challenged ORIT.

According to Christian labor sources the conference was attended by some 140 trade union leaders from the entire Latin American area. The following excerpts from the "Workers Charter for the Liberation and Unity of Latin American Peoples" which has drawn up by the conference constitutes a good overall summary of the ideas which Emilio Máspero had been fervently declaiming within CLASC itself.[16]

The preamble notes that the workers of Latin America who represent the majority of the people are "the victims of imperialism, capitalism, internal colonialism, and their consequences of underdevelopment, poverty and national disunity." The charter insists that a "New Society" must be created which "can only be born of conscious and concerted action to take control over the economic, social and political future." It is asserted that "development is not achieved by highly-qualified technical experts, nor by means of official governmental measures, nor through dealing and bargaining between individual politicians or parties nor by instructions and assistance sent from foreign countries to the Latin American continent." It is further indicated that "development cannot be imposed from outside with systems and ideologies that correspond to foreign situations and interests (but) authentic development should originate

1784384

within the country itself and entails an essential and thorough transformation of the way people think, live, act and possess." In order to bring about the creation of the required new men of the new society whole nations must be mobilized and a revolutionary mystique created. This is necessary for the carrying out of the "necessary" and "irreplaceable" method of revolution to obtain the new objects. The conference denounced "the various processes of capitalist developments that are colonizing Latin America," the new forms of governmental-sponsored or private national or international projects by means of which "the traditional forces of power are trying to reinforce the position of national oligarchies by a system of "super capitalism" which inevitably favors the intervention of foreign monopolies. Again denunciation was sounded against the "ingenious doctrine of participation" by means of which it is asserted that the "neo-capitalists are endeavoring to make the Latin American trade union movement into an alien and docile agent for transmitting governmental directives." The Charter sought the establishment of an ideology of national and Latin American development which will furnish a non-capitalist way of attaining the total development of our countries.

The Charter went on to assert that an overall unity of all of Latin American people and countries "which will stress Latin Americanism instead of Pan-Americanism must develop." The "most constant factor" which historically and at this hour stands in opposition to a Latin American union "has always been and still is the *predominating influence of the United States* whose interests and politics play a role in every field of Latin American life. "*Revolutionary Latin American institutions*" must replace "effectively and permanently the Pan-American system . . . " Current attempts at Latin American integration have only economic targets in mind, their methods "are of the liberal capitalist type, benefiting only the present groupings in power." These current integration efforts are made by "governments that in general are unrepresentative, that reflect a thought and ideology alien to Latin America and her people and "which represents in face the final stage of the consolidation of capitalist imperialism in Latin America."

The achievement of Latin American solidarity is the first task, but the present world situation means that this Latin American solidarity is part of a process of the unity that is developing between "all of the workers and peoples of the Third World. This unity constitutes a single front (Third World solidarity) which contains enough power and strength to demand substantial changes in the relations between states and in the functioning of international practice. From Third World solidarity it is hoped that *World Solidarity* will develop and with it the understanding that is necessary for the peace and progress for all the peoples of the world without discrimination."

The Charter closes by turning from the world scene to return to the western hemisphere. It warns of the *Punte del Este's* "unpopular projects" which "plan the beginning of the neo-capitalist process of Latin American integration . . . The workers of Latin America proclaim their decision to oppose this process of development and integration with all their strength, for it does not correspond to the ideals and expectations of our peoples." Calling upon all to join "in the fight for liberation" reasserting that the unity of all the workers of Latin America is the "vanguard of the organized people" the Charter closes with the italicized statement that "the Organized People and United Workers will have the last word."

While the preamble to this Charter stated that its subscribers had disassociated themselves temporarily from conflicting and dividing "ideological, religious, political or other divergencies" the Charter itself was in keeping with Máspero's views of what constituted the mission of the then-named Christian trade unionism. Christian trade unionism viewed by Jáuregui and numerous democratic labor leaders all over the world with suspicion as being in some fashion a Church instrument, carried the meaning for Máspero of a force for a sweeping program of socioeconomic and political change which finds its genesis in the Christian social philosophy and ethic. That social ethic he argued demands a revolution in today's Latin America. In order to achieve the dignity of man, to create the condition in which men can fulfill themselves in Latin American society as loving creatures and develop their best selves individually and socially, a change that cannot be gradual or superficial must take place.

The Christian revolutionary doctrine, unlike the ethic of capitalism and communism, does not base its appeal fundamentally upon materialistic forces, for in practice they lead to the control of the masses of men in the interest of an economic elite (capitalism) or a political elite (communism). Demanding sweeping changes the Christian revolutionary does so in the interest of the spiritually-oriented human being. From the Christian view of man as a human being made in God's image and likeness with an immortal soul, the humanistic attention to man's condition on earth as a creature of God may be extracted without accepting the narrower theological implications. Such a view is for the common good and may be accepted by all men of good will.

Thus the ethic of Christian trade union position is not a narrowly religious position but originates in social Christian inspiration that reaches beyond any particular creed. Christian trade unionism, according to its adherents, welcomes all like-minded revolutionaries no matter what their religious (or lack of religious) beliefs. Here is an inspiration for people in search of an ideology with which to combat communism, capitalism, dictatorship of various kinds; an ideology that in a world of fiercely combating ideologies offers the inspiration and guidelines of a revolutionary spiritual humanism.

Máspero repeatedly underscored the importance of this Christian ethic, taking pains to enunciate its validity as an inspirational call to all interested revolutionaries, which is separate from any church or church-sponsored control or affiliation. Repeatedly he emphasized it as a doctrine devoid of any "confessionalism," standing apart from any ecclesiastical authority of lay Catholic action group.[17] The CLASC leader made these reiterations because of "certain Americans" (including Latin Americans also, like Jáuregui)

who choose to oppose us refer to "secular" trade unionism as if Christian trade unionism, by contrast, were clerical and denominational. We *also* constitute a secular trade unionism, but not a neutral trade unionism. We take our inspiration from that which, we are convinced, is the most sure and best solution for the present drama of Latin American workers and peasants, oppressed by injustice and hunger, and misery but desirous of finally seeing the light of their social redemption.[18]

In *CLASC: The Voice of Revolutionary Trade Unionism in Latin America*, the monthly journal of the organization that appeared after Máspero took command, the ideology was presented in a militant popular extremist style. It exposed the perfidious actions of American government, business, and labor in the interests of American capitalism that it asserted were practiced against the Latin American people. Among the Latin American trade union leaders who deliver "without scruples all the interests of the workers and peoples of Latin America to Yankee imperialism and international capitalism" Arturo Jáuregui was prominently cited. He was identified as "General Secretary of the ORIT (the free trade unionism that cooperates the most with all the fascist and gorilla attempts of Latin America)."[19]

Ideology–The CLAT

As has been stated and briefly explained, the conversion of CLASC to CLAT meant the continuation of a missionary ideology in an even more militant fashion. Let us now look a bit more closely at the belief system and strategy and tactics expressed at the transformation Congress at Caracas in November 1971, and in Máspero's speech at Mérida during July of the following year. This scrutiny reveals the overall aggressive posture and the strengthening of the belief system itself in a further elaboration of older ideas, and in the introduction and explanation of others. There is a reinforcement of the by now familiar themes of anti-capitalism, anti-communism, and pro-socialism in general and in their particular and manifold applications to Latin America. To this is added an explanation of the singular kind of class struggle which Máspero envisions as an essential means for the workers' liberation, a linking of the workers' movement with the Black Power forces in Latin America and a further identification with the struggles of the native Indian populations. An increasingly aggressive anticlerical position is joined with a delineation—mostly a warning—of religion's role in aiding the workers in the social struggle.

Furthermore, Máspero explains in some detail the manner in which ubiquitous capitalism and neocapitalism have penetrated the formal and voluntary institutions and groupings in society creating obstacles for the workers to overcome. Education, family, religion, governmental legislation, political parties—all, he observes, have been infected in one fashion or other by capitalism at the expense of the workers. And he warns the workers that so-called "reforms" are the modern means of seeking to integrate them into the exploiting society.

The nature of this continuing interest of the CLAT and its leader in animating the workers with a guiding doctrine, the pains taken in spelling out the argument of the ideology, and its tone and direction may be seen—to take just two examples—in Máspero's views relating to the class struggle, and those concerned with clericalism and the role of religion in today's Latin America.

Like the Marxists, Máspero sees the class struggle brought about by a profiteering economic order which divides society into irreducibly antagonistic classes. Like Marxists, as well as others, he views capitalist society as deeply violent. Like the Marxists, too, the class struggle is seen as the means by which the workers will free themselves from exploitation and enter the road to socialism. But Máspero, nevertheless, is opposed to the Marxist interpretation of the class struggle. He says that Marx himself and Marxism gives an interpretation that is applicable to such dictatorial models as that of today's Soviet society. Marxism's view of the class struggle, he argues, does not agree in any way with the aspirations of a genuine communitarian socialism, or with the genuine aspirations for liberation of the Latin American people.

Máspero asserts that the class struggle is, to be sure, a crucially important means to the workers' success, at this time in history, and there can be no neutrality with regard to it. One must stand with the oppressors or the oppressed. At the same time he argues that this vital means is not an absolute, it is not an end in itself. As a means it must serve the moral values of the workers who struggle for the new, better social order. It is not the creator of those moral values.

Máspero contrasts this view of the primacy of moral values in the relation to class conflict with that of Lenin in which morality is subordinated to the class struggle of the proletariat. Marxism, concludes the CLAT leader, subordinates moral values to the development of history and by refusing the right of the moral conscience to judge history destroys the autonomous action of the workers' movement and the values which animate the movement. Marxism thus converts the movement into a totally alienated instrument.

It is not hate that strengthens the workers in their struggle, according to Máspero. Hate, he says, is destructive of the revolutionary process. He calls hate and resentment the weapons of mediocrities. On the contrary, the inspiring emotion is that of love. Increasingly, Máspero tells his audience, he is convinced that all true revolutionaries see in revolution an act of love. The revolution must be made, is made, in the name of man's humanization.

Máspero quotes from statements attributed to Ché Guevara in support of the view that love is the guiding sentiment of the true revolutionary. Such, he says, was the view of a man who preferred armed struggle in order to achieve the liberation of Latin America. Máspero, the anti-Marxist, here uses the illustration of a Marxist charismatic folk hero to many Latin Americans, an advocate of violence as a weapon of the class struggle who, he says, nevertheless did not forget the great inspiration of love in his armed conflict for freedom.

In conclusion the CLAT leader reaffirms that today's capitalist society reveals the reality of the class struggle that the workers experience every day. A genuine love for man, he says, will push one towards a clear historical choice and militant commitment with the cause of the oppressed. It will drive towards a final conflict against the capitalist system. It will furnish a creative and original force for the construction of a new society desired by the workers. Communitarian socialism must, he avows, draw out the theoretical and practical conclusions which arise from the class struggle within the capitalist society. It must realize that the workers are the most forceful and decisive agents of history and the fundamental motor of the anti-capitalist battle and of the process of constructing the new society.[20]

Such, in brief, is Máspero's exposition of the class struggle. It constitutes his particular version of a non-Marxist, anti-capitalist call to revolution. It exemplifies his deep interest in ideology, its importance in arming the workers, and the lengths to which he will go in examining ideological questions. His views concerning clericalism and the position of religion in the contemporary Latin American society further reveal his concern in these regards.

The picture of Máspero that emerges from his admonitions to the workers concerning clericalism and religion is one of an extreme left-wing Christian socialist. He asserts a flat uncompromising opposition to clericalism in any shape or form. Looking at religion and the churches, but especially the Catholic Church in Latin America, his emphasis is on the critical side. While he praises those forces within the churches that today constitute a revolutionary element for their anti-capitalistic, pro-worker position, his greatest concern is to remind his adherents of what was the major historic role of the Church in Latin America and to warn them of the dangers from the churches in contemporary times. As the Church was the spiritual and moral arm of feudalism and capitalism in the past, so in many ways the churches today, with the modernization of capitalism, he asserts, are serving neo-capitalism. Organized religion—along with various other institutions which have inculcated "reforms"—are beguiling, or trying to beguile, the workers. These so-called "reforms" are really a different way of sustaining the "reformed" capitalism and of integrating the workers into the new neo-capitalist society.

Of the various kinds of paternalism within the capitalist society which operate to help control the workers, the paternalism of clericalism and neo-clericalism, says Máspero, is one of the most persistent and dangerous. For it is a paternalism in which the will of God is manipulated by those claiming to be the agents of God. In warning the workers Máspero asserts that the left-wing clericals who seek to monopolize the revolutionary truths are as dangerous as the conservative right-wing. These left-wing clericals who, he asserts, are as dogmatic and secretarian as their right-wing opponents threaten the autonomy and personality of the workers' movement.

On the positive side the CLAT leader notes with approval the processes of revision and radical change going on in the churches today that help as never before the cause of the workers, and which are critical of capitalism. There is a need for support from spiritual and religious forces in order to bring about freedom which is decisive for the total development of Latin America. The workers must, he says, take upon themselves the duty of aiding and abetting in all ways such progressive religious forces. But it bears repeating that the burden of Máspero's message is to proclaim eternal vigilance on the part of the workers against clerical paternalism. Wherever clericalism in any form (right, center, left) is encountered it must be denounced and fought. By so doing not only will the workers maintain their movement's autonomy but they will be helping the churches free themselves from totally negative and false positions.[21]

Máspero's ideological posture as regards the class struggle and religion shows the essence of his kind of radical Christian socialism. The ideology posits a class struggle in which the workers victimized by an exploiting capitalism play their historic role as the class that overthrows the oppressive society and opens the door to socialism. But Marxism is rejected as being dictatorial and for refusing to moral values the creative role in the shaping of the conflict. Christianity helps contribute to the moral position, but the control of the workers' movement itself is in secular hands. Contemporary radical and progressive forces within the churches are welcomed, but the predominant attitude towards religion in its relations with capitalism is one of suspicion.

When Máspero speaks of love and not hate as the driving emotional force of the class struggle he cites Fidelista, Ché Guevara, an advocate of violence in support of his own emphasis upon the need for love as the mark of the true revolutionary. So, too, in a certain sense Padre Camillo Torres, Jacques Chonchol, and Salvador Allende could be said to be Máspero's "strategic" companions. And thus one can better comprehend Máspero's and the CLAT's willingness to, on occasion, advocate cooperation even with Marxists when it is felt that the ends for the cooperation are the same. This extremist Christian radicalism animates the entire CLAT ideology. But the root was already there in the CLASC. And the source of the root is Máspero.

Summary

In sum the conflicting views indicate one leader, Jáuregui, attempting to bring about what he regards as revolutionary changes by acting within the framework of the present political and social system where such action is at all possible. The rival leader Máspero, has virtually written off the possibility that meaningful change can be brought about in most of Latin America through the present institutions.

Jáuregui, leading a more stabilized and conservative (he would say "more responsible") organization, advocates a more gradual approach as the better way to obtaining an eventual revolution. Well aware that a reality of Latin American politics has been for the most part a politics of accommodation and that defiance and confrontation of the powerful interest groups can be a dangerous risk, Jáuregui takes the difficult road of a gradualist "revolution by consent" within the system. He still maintains a belief in the worth of the populist parties in advancing the workers cause. Opposed to the older type of capitalism he has been an advocate of the changing, more liberal type of capitalism. In recent years he has spoken in favor of democratic socialism. In recent years, too, he has given increasing attention to the peasantry, who where organized have been more militant revolutionaries than their earlier organized city brothers, and to the importance of an ideology. He seeks to advise his autonomous older organization to make a revolution through evolution in company with those who are all at least in the camp of the non-totalitarians. Jáuregui is engaged in the hard task of working within the system in order to eventually transcend it.

Emilio Máspero's stance, in contrast, is that of a militant extremist, the advocate of sweeping change. He believes in a fresh beginning under new conditions. Máspero has placed his workers' movement in the vanguard of those seeking a new society. He appears to view the CLAT's primary task as the uniting of all workers—using the term in its broadest sense—who are anxious to advance the Third World position between capitalism and communism in Latin America. Máspero has been more the ideologist than is his rival. He has been more preoccupied with the construction of a rationale, a weapon of justification for overthrowing the old and providing a vision of the new society. Máspero is much more given to avowals and explanations of his particular ideas of the necessary revolution than is Jáuregui.

Like many other revolutionists of different ideological persuasion, Máspero stresses the importance of the developing areas of today's world to the making of a new world order. He rejects what he sees as the attempts of the imperialist Soviet Union and the imperialist United States to control the world and, of course, he views the kind of trade unionism operating in each of these super-powers as unsatisfactory and harmful to the developing areas of the "Third World." As for his own section of the world he is extremely sensitive to what he sees as the decidedly foreign and dangerous consequences of the ORIT's close relationship with North American trade unionists. For Máspero only *latinos* can successfully build trade unions and develop that essential ideology which will unite the workers to make the revolution.

Jáuregui is the pragmatic statesman advancing the ideal of democratic trade unionism through the institutions of the actual society while his rival is more the audacious revolutionary intellectual engagé, who seeks to transcend the present society as necessary for the building of a new order of the "Third Way" founded upon the universal inspiration of Christian humanism. The final chapter of this study will analyze the strengths and weaknesses in the ideas of each leader in their operationalization. Before turning to that task the study will assist in obtaining a fuller comprehension of this rivalry, by examining the views of these rivals concerning the United States as these views are expressed in reaction to specific U.S. actions in Latin America.

4

Conflicting Perspectives II: Attitudes Toward the United States

In making a more detailed examination of each labor leader's reactions to the various governmental and extra-governmental activities of the "Giant of the North" it is helpful to begin with certain basic questions. What is the view of each man concerning U.S.-Latin American relationships in general? What is the view of each concerning the capitalist-democracy of the United States? What are their attitudes towards what passes for the U.S. government's foreign policy affecting Latin America—the many-sided aspects of it with regard to communism, how it affects trade unions, the crucial matter of intervention, the United States-Latin American relations in the Organization of American States?

In each case a different perception is held. The ORIT leader has always believed in *latinos* taking a cooperative attitude towards the United States whenever this is possible. From his pragmatic viewpoint *el coloso del norte*, whether represented by government, labor, or business in a definite sense is bound to play a predominant role in hemispheric politics. This is simply a fact of life. Whether or not the *yanquis* are likable, the *latinos* will have to in one fashion or other be on close terms with the government and people of their powerful omnipresent northern neighbor. Therefore, it is best for those who would serve Latin American interests to join with the United States in cooperative efforts affecting the hemisphere, to seek United States aid and assistance where such help is beneficial to Latin America and does not compromise Latin American *dignidad* or Latin American sovereignty.

Such a policy, as Jáuregui knows very well, is at times particularly difficult to carry out. Due to the various circumstances, the basic one being the vast differences in power possessed by the "big neighbor" in relation to the others, there is bound to be friction. In relations between governments, business, and labor activities, controversies will arise. All this Jáuregui freely acknowledges. He believes, however, that despite the difficulties a policy of cooperation and working together is, at bottom, the best one.

Emilio Máspero's perception stands in sharp contrast. While at times distinguishing between the people of the United States and their leaders in governments, labor and business, there runs throughout Máspero's perception a definitely pessimistic note as concerns the possibility or the desirability of close working relationships between the United States and its *latino* hemispheric neighbors. History, he feels, substantiates the truth that the "big neighbor" has sought to make economic colonies of the smaller *latino* countries, has intervened in their affairs when it wished. Despite periodic expressions of the need for cooperation, exemplified, for example, in support for Pan-Americanism, *el coloso* has sought and continues to seek to use the weaker countries to further the policies of the United States at the expense of their own interests. The United States, a competing imperialist power, sought to push Latin America into its cold war disputes with the Soviet Union and the Communist world. It openly intervened with armed force in Cuba and the Dominican Republic.

Moreover, it is important says Máspero, in effect, to remember that ethic and cultural roots of *yanquis* and *latinos* are decidedly different. Those roots have produced different societies with different values. This does not mean that the peoples and governments cannot, or ought not to live in peace and mutual respect. They can and should. Unfortunately what passes for friendly relations and respect between the United States and the Latin countries, at bottom has too often in the past been the result of the Latin neighbors being in some fashion actually colonies of their "big neighbor." Past and present experience has proven that any kind of partnership between the United States and its Latin hemispheric neighbors resembles that between a fox and chicken.

Jáuregui has displayed a definite appreciation of what may be called the United States' liberal-capitalistic democratic way. This is not to say that as one still influenced by *Aprismo* he has been devoid of sympathy for a form of socialist democracy. Indeed in recent years an increasing acceptance of such socialism is evident in his observations. But he has over the years also spoken favorably of a liberal capitalist "free-enterprise" society. He has expressed a personal view in the past that a liberal progressive form of free enterprise is helpful to free labor and has at least on one occasion stated that the ORIT is at times a champion of free enterprise and a bulwark against drives to discredit the capitalist form of society.[1] He appreciates the advances that American workers have made under the capitalist democracy of the United States. At times, over the years, he has expressed hopes for such developments to come about in Latin America—to the degree it is possible there.

At the same time, he by no means sees the ORIT itself as solely the champion of liberal capitalism, and he knows that future Latin American political-economic developments will move in ways that protagonists of free enterprise capitalism in the United States may find difficult to accept.[2]

The ORIT leader's *latino* critics, of course, interpret Jáuregui's views vis à vis the progressive type of U.S. capitalism and enlightened American businessmen as proof that he and the ORIT are the tools of United States imperialism. His *latino* defenders obviously see the whole picture quite differently.[3]

Emilio Máspero has paid tribute (if in minor key, it is nevertheless on record) to the liberal-capitalistic democracy of the North. But he is emphatic that this type of democracy is not his way and that with all of its accomplishments it is judged wanting. While admitting that the present liberal capitalism is superior to that prevailing in the earlier industrial era of the United States, he finds it inadequate and harmful both at home and (particularly) abroad. To Máspero, liberal free-enterprise capitalism, or "neo-capitalism" cannot hide the important fact that whatever advantages it has brought to the workers the basic decisions controlling the economy rest with the capitalists. Thus, Máspero would not, as has American labor, accept a revised capitalism—a so-called "people's capitalism." Moreover, he, of course, believes that in Latin America free-enterprise capitalism is "one of the most formidable forces" in opposition to the betterment of the majority of peasants and city workers.[4]

Máspero is willing to accept the fact that the North American workers have benefited by and accept the present capitalism which they helped to shape. At the same time he asserts that the liberal-capitalistic democratic America has contributed its share to the development of the cold war. Unfortunately, in their belief in democracy and capitalism the majority of American labor leaders became cold war patriots. These democratic labor chieftains led the rank and file unionists into supporting U.S. cold war aggressions. Furthermore, he believes that the linking of democracy with capitalism is wrong and that doing so has hurt democracy's cause in Latin America.[5]

Máspero's attitude toward capitalistic United States, then, is that which might be expected from one who in the first place has little sympathy with capitalism per se. When he explains the way in which he believes capitalism has been practiced by the United States in Latin America and by Latin American entrepreneurs themselves, this antagonism to capitalism which affects his perception of the United States is understandable.

The respective views of the two men concerning United States government policy as it relates to Latin America make clearer the basis friendliness of Jáuregui to the United States and his rival's much more critical attitude. This may be illustrated in their views towards such important matters as the Alliance for Progress, U.S. policies on communism, the question of U.S. interventions in Latin America in the last decades, U.S. policies in the Organization of American States, and the U.S. government's posture concerning trade unionism in Latin America.

The Alliance for Progress

Jáuregui was an early enthusiastic supporter of the Alliance for Progress and continues to defend it. He joined repeatedly with his friends (as well as those with whom he disagreed) in the AIFLD (American Institute for Free Labor Development) to carry the "Alpro" message throughout Latin America. He was a tireless worker in seeking that labor's voice be heard in the highest councils of those who shape the living image of the Alliance. In innumerable ways, in public and private meetings, he has carried on this task. At times here, as in other matters relating to the United States, Jáuregui took upon himself the role of constructive critic. Believing in the importance of the Alliance he is emphatic in asserting that he has always underscored the Latin American side of this partnership with the strong northern neighbor. His view is that despite its lacks, the Alliance served a positive good. He, therefore, worked to bring about what he saw as improvements in the "Alpro"—improving labor's role to one of a decision-participant in the top management circles of the Alliance. "We hope and fight for that end," he told the author some years ago.[6]

Emilio Máspero, in contrast, has long since turned away from the Alliance. For a time, in the beginning, he hoped some basic good would come of it. But he soon became disillusioned. In his early attempts to bring the CLASC into participation in the operation of the Alliance Máspero was, typically, less diplomatic than Jáuregui. His demands violated the processes by which the U.S. Congress grants approval to foreign expenditures. Evidently he did not care if those demands were an affront to the U.S. procedures of administering those funds.[7]

Máspero has for some years made the by now quite familiar criticism of Alliance program, namely that not enough publicity was given to the fact that it is not an exclusive North American program, and that the contributions made by the *yanquis* were marked so that in order to use them Latin Americans would be forced to buy American goods and equipment or machinery, whether or not they thought that such American products were the best available. The Alliance, he says, has benefited the upper class of Latin America more than the masses whom it presumably aims at helping. Indeed he feels that in practice the Alliance helped support or install dictatorships in Latin America and abetted violence. He also saw in the Alliance an effort on the part of the U.S. government to accomplish what he charges the AFL-CIO is seeking also to accomplish, namely, the forcing of North American values upon *latinos*. The wealthy *yanquis* seem to feel that by spending money they can "reculturalize" a civilization which is far different, and in some respects superior to their own. They are, he asserts, failing and will continue to fail.

For some time Máspero has labeled the Alliance an agency of discrimination against trade unionism in Latin America which the United States dislikes. Moreover, he asserts, "Alpro" gave aid to countries which (in opposition to the very provisions of the Alliance) did not make the reforms that presumably were prerequisite to receiving such aid. Thus, not only has the *Alianza* obstructed the social revolution which it was created to assist, but it became an instrument of American imperialism throughout Latin America, particularly where labor unions are concerned.[8]

These criticisms of the Alliance have been made in the "grand scale" of the radical democrat. In truth Máspero today has long since finished with mere criticism and passed to the attack. He understood that the Alliance was really to be an instrument of peaceful social revolution. It failed to live up to its promise and became an obstacle to that essential change.

U.S. Policy and Communism

We turn now to the matter of U.S. policy concerning communism in Latin America. Once more the differing attitudes of the rival leaders emerge. The leader of the ORIT has in general been a firm supporter of the United States anti-Communist policies. The leader of the CLAT has been a critic of those policies. Both men are avowed critics of communism, but Máspero, as was earlier observed, sees a greater danger to Latin America from U.S. imperialism than he does from either foreign or domestic communism.

Given Jáuregui's fundamentally friendly view of the United States and his orthodox *Aprista* beliefs, it is not surprising that he has exhibited less fear of U.S. imperialism, of Soviet imperialism, and of communism. He has supported U.S. anti-Communist policy in Latin America. Recently a concern that perhaps the United States has been too massively preoccupied with the danger of communism in Latin America has been evidenced in his private conversations. But one finds very little such criticism expressed in public from press or platform. On the contrary, he has applauded the United States' alertness to what he continues to see as the dangers from foreign and/or domestic communism and has supported American efforts to combat communism throughout the hemisphere. His record, here, shows that he (while voicing some criticism) has had a overall sympathetic understanding concerning the U.S. government's direct or indirect interventions in Guatemala, Cuba, and the Dominican Republic.[9]

As has been indicated, Jáuregui was one of the Latin American "Founding Fathers" of the ORIT in 1951. This organization, mainly inspired by North American union leaders with the blessings of their government, set out to expose and destroy Communist influence among Latin American workers. The ORIT was mainly responsible for the demise of the once powerful CTAL, which it exposed as a Communist front organization.[10]

The ORIT leader continues to view communism as a menace to the security of the hemisphere and especially to the health of democratic trade unionist growth in Latin America. He knows that in Latin America conditions are such as might predispose the workers towards accepting Communist explanations of their sorry lot. He approves of U.S. government and U.S. labor support of people, policies and programs which are aimed against or seek to block the influence of *Fidelistas*, of pro-Russian Latin American Communists, pro-Chinese Communists, or of the influence of any variety of Marxist-Leninist and fellow travelers throughout Latin America. His answer to those who cite this as again proof that he and the ORIT are tools of the United States is in effect this: Joining with those who fight a totalitarian theory and a practice which makes people, and specifically unions, creatures of the state, is something that should merit not criticism, but congratulations. He believes that any Latin American labor leader should appreciate the overall good in the United States policy of opposition to the Marxist-Leninist enemy in its various forms. Criticisms of United States policy, whenever necessary, should he feels be made concerning tactics, not the ends. The enemy is too powerful to do otherwise. However, he also asserts labor's independent right to seek its own destiny. He affirms that he has insisted this right must always be respected by any anti-Communist elements who come to power through deposing pro-Communist or "fellow-traveling" governments.[11]

Máspero, of course, sees the United States policy towards communism in Latin America in an entirely different light. He sees it with the eyes of one who as a *latino* fears U.S. imperialism more than he does the interventions of Moscow, or of the *Fidelistas*, which he has also condemned. He also regards American policy as a part of the cold war and he is not interested in helping either side in that conflict.

Máspero is aware that communism may appear to the anxiety-ridden capitalist Americans as an omnipresent threat to their freedom and even national security. It is somewhat understandable, therefore, why *they* should be so concerned about it.

He believes, however, that to the majority of Latin Americans the dangers from communism do not appear as great as the harm they have suffered from other sources. Communism he feels is more frequently viewed by Latins as one alternative to capitalism—a possible alternative to the economic and social order which in one form or other has for many generations exploited the Latin American masses. He knows that for the most part the history of Communist activities in Latin America has been one of revolutionary rhetoric. In practice Communist parties, when they were not harried by the authorities, were engaged in making political deals with the authorities who looked upon the Communists with no great concern. Máspero, to be sure, is critical of communism as a highly authoritarian political system based on a materialism that blinds it to the primacy of man as a human being. At the same time he does not believe that communism in practice in today's Latin America poses any great danger. The greater danger relating to communism comes from U.S. exaggerated fears and U.S. actions in the hemisphere as part of the cold war.

To a person of such views it is patent that the United States primarily is responsible for bringing the cold war to the Latin part of the Western Hemisphere. Máspero resents this intervention. He seeks a society that is neither capitalist, nor Communist. He repeatedly has asserted that he wants to keep Latin America out of the cold war and the cold war out of Latin America. In that conflict he has opposed both sides although, for reasons already stated, the greater weight of his opposition is turned against United States policies. He believes the American anti-Communist program in Latin America is dangerous and immoral. The overbearing U.S. concern with stopping communism leads, he says, to helping dictators of the Right. It seeks to focus the attentions of Latins on a kind of omnipresent threatening image when the threat is much greater from the United States. The United States, he feels, has also sought to bribe needy countries to accept U.S. policies. Actions of top American diplomats have frequently given offense to Latin American sensibilities by their neglect of matters of greater interest to the Latins in favor of a primary concern with fighting communism.

Thus, for Máspero, the American anti-Communist policy has lacked intelligence—irritating rather than convincing those to whom it is addressed. This American negative "anti-revolutionary" policy of overconcern with communism also blocks the political and economic changes Latin America must make if it is to achieve the new social order which Máspero seeks.[12] Despite its stupidity, danger, and immorality the United States has persisted in its negative policy.

U.S. Intervention in Latin America

Primarily responsible for making Latin America a cold war terrain the United States, moreover, according to Máspero, has revived its old bad practice of a most dangerous and arrogant direct interventionism in Latin American affairs.

This burning question of intervention underscores again the contrasting perspectives of the two rival labor leaders. Latin American nations themselves historically have periodically intervened in each other's backyards and have on occasion even gone to war with each other. In principle, however, they are as one in their support of formal declarations binding the hemispheric powers in opposition to intervention. Of course, the particular intervention that matters most to them is the one at times indulged in by *el coloso del Norte* directly—or indirectly.

How do our two rival labor leaders approach this momentous problem? It can be taken for granted that as Latin Americans they are opposed to U.S. intervention as a matter of principle. What must be spelled out is the way they interpreted their belief in actual situations—i.e., the attacks on Cuba in 1961 and the Dominican revolt in 1965. For obvious reasons Jáuregui was under great pressure in those days, since he led an organization half of whose members belong to North American affiliates. These affiliates represent, by far, the wealthiest and the most advanced trade unions within the ORIT. The voice of the AFL-CIO (and the "concurring" AIFLD) is bound to carry weight with the ORIT's top management. What, then, is the attitude on these instances of intervention by a labor leader with such close connections with the *yanquis*?

The ORIT leader declares that whatever his relations with the North Americans he is always first of all a Latin American. He has spent his life in the labor movement trying to better the lot of the Latin American worker, and in asserting the significance and dignity of Latin America before the world. Speaking for himself and his Latin fellows sums up his attitude towards his powerful North American coworkers thusly, "We are friends, but not colonials."

The very delicate matter of U.S. intervention in Cuba and the Dominican Republic he believes when the facts are fully comprehended can be explained as in keeping with Latin American interests.

As one who has repeatedly condemned what he believes to be the infamous and totalitarian treatment of the Cuban workers by the Castro regime, Jáuregui was predisposed from the start to applaud U.S. forceful opposition to the Cuban Fidelista-Communist state. He is a leader who used his organization to support American policy of intervention against Cuba, including the acceptance of the ill-fated and misguided "Bay of Pigs" venture in 1961.[13] He was, moreover, a leader in the ORIT's own particular boycott of Cuba formed in effect as a supplement to the blockade of Cuba by the United States. It was under his direction that an ORIT "Action Committee Against Cuban Communist Tyranny" was formed in 1965 to halt the flow of goods and services to Castro's Cuba. The activities of this committee extended beyond the boycott of ships of nations trading with Cuba. It included a vast publicity program with an extensive variety of communication channels and a special mandate to keep "the ICFTU, the AFL-CIO, the international trade secretariats, the ILO, the UN and the OAS and the pertinent national governments informed of such actions against the Cuban targets as it deems appropriate."[14]

One could multiply the examples of the ORIT's consistent efforts to oppose the Castro regime and Jáuregui's energetic leadership in expediting them. These efforts support the general United States policy carried out by the Department of State. It must be remembered that the U.S. State Department's relations with the AFL-CIO (the most powerful member in the ORIT) on labor matters and foreign policy is an intimate one. It would appear, however, that the contact is not the simple one where the powerful labor group and the government agency work hand-in-hand in Latin America, with the AFL-CIO carrying out the programs approved by the Department of State. AFL-CIO specialists on labor affairs it may be assumed greatly contribute to the State Department's policies in Latin America concerning labor matters. While each powerful corporate group is opposed to communism, the never tiring continuous anti-Communist and anti-Fidelistic Cuban posture of the AFL-CIO might be said to exceed that of U.S. government policymakers. Thus, within the realm of U.S. policy concerning Latin America and specifically Cuba, and the realm of the ORIT policy that Jáuregui supports and leads, the United States government and the ORIT and its secretary general, are said by their critics to be expediting suggestions that often originate with the AFL-CIO.

Jáuregui's answer to this criticism is as follows: He himself, and the overwhelming majority of the *latinos* in the ORIT, are emphatically opposed to communism. Their opposition pre-dates the founding of the ORIT. These Latin Americans have no need of their AFL-CIO brethren pressuring them to oppose the Fidelista Cuban tyranny. They freely join with their fellows of the AFL-CIO in opposition to Castro. They, therefore, support in general the U.S. policy against a country that they, too, like the Americans, feel is tyrannical and a Soviet satellite. It is all the more commendable that they so act because they do so in full knowledge of the attacks that they will be subjected to by their critics who play upon traditional Latin American anti-Yankee sentiment. But in their own voluntary hatred of tyranny, they are no more the tools of U.S. foreign policy than they are of AFL-CIO anti-Communist policy.

Jáuregui, moreover, is well aware of another belief fostered by his critics—namely that in attacking Castro and sympathizing in general with the U.S. policy he appears to be fighting a revolutionary nationalistic, socialistic movement in its own backyard, the kind of movement that seems in many ways to be a part of Latin America's future. Jáuregui, however, believes that Castro's socialism is not democratic socialism, but tyranny. His hope is that time may provide the solution, that Castro will in the end fail as his dictatorship becomes more apparent and more and more Cubans and Latin Americans realize that he betrayed the original revolution he sparked against the previous tyrant, Batista. Then ORIT's policy, a pragmatic one, but fused by its opposition to totalitarianism, will prove basically correct. As he puts it "the original democratic goals of Castro's revolution remain those of the ORIT, the United States and the Alliance for Progress—but Castro, who betrayed those goals and his totalitarian regime, must go."[15]

Let us turn to Jáuregui's attitude concerning the United States intervention in the Dominican Republic. In the early spring of 1965 a conflict erupted in that republic between the forces of the primarily right-wing militarists, and the popular elements under the command of a young colonel, a supporter of the former president (at the time in exile), democratic socialist Juan Bosch. The United States Marines were dispatched to the Dominican Republic presumably to aid in the evacuation of American citizens and protect American properties. However, they stayed on and soon placed themselves between the contending native combatants in a manner advantageous to the militarists. It then began to appear that the marines' presence reflected the Johnson administration's deep concern over the possibility of another Communist take-over in Latin America. That administration was assuring the Americans of the United States that there would be no "second Cuba" in the other Americas. Later the U.S. unilateral action was presumably softened by the OAS's (Organization of American States) belated dispatch of Latin American military contingents to the troubled area. Eventually things were quieted down and all the foreign soldiers left. A caretaker government prepared for the later elections which were to produce as president the meek and pious Joaquin Balaguer, a former rector of the University of Santo Domingo.

The American intervention caused an uproar throughout Latin America and among liberal circles within the United States. The ORIT and its secretary general were excoriated by their various critics for having again played the United States game. Jáuregui and the ORIT before, during, and after the internal conflict it was charged had acted to obstruct and defeat Juan Bosch.

The situation in the Dominican Republic was all the more complicated by the rivalry that had developed after 1962, during Bosch's short-lived administration, between the ORIT and the CLASC. The ORIT had sent its representatives to the Dominican Republic after the assassination of Trujillo in 1961. Working in the midst of several rival international labor representatives and those from the trade unions from Latin America and the United States they influenced greatly those who in 1962 formed the *Confederación Nacional de Trabajadores* (CNTL) and affiliated with the ORIT. The CNTI, or CONATRAL, was the largest single trade union body in the country.

In 1962, also as a result of CLASC activity, *Confederación Autonoma de Sindicatos Christianos* was established. This grew rapidly and by 1964 was challenging the CNTL for primacy among the central labor organizations in the country. It was one of the most viable trade union groups among the comparatively few such affiliated with the then CLASC. Here, in other words, was a CLASC local rival of the local ORIT affiliate able to compete on an equal basis for the loyalty of the trade unionists in the country, a rare occurrence.[16]

When the United States intervened in the spring of 1965 the Dominican unions affiliated with the ORIT stood aside. They had taken a neutral position in the civil conflict refusing to participate in the general strike the pro-Bosch elements called in protesting military brutality. Later CONATRAL denounced the revolution as "Communist inspired." It also publicly thanked Washington for sending the marines. This attitude contrasted sharply with that expressed by the CLASC affiliate and the pro-Bosch unions.

ORIT's affiliates' actions were interpreted in several quarters as constituting ORIT support of the unilateral U.S. intervention. Later, in the elections held in 1966, the ORIT unions supported the U.S. preferred candidate, the successful Balaguer, for whom the AFL-CIO had expressed its strong approval. The CLASC unions and those influenced by the small Communist movement were among those who shared in the unexpectedly emphatic defeat of democratic socialist Juan Bosch. The ORIT, once again, was charged by its critics with being a pro-Yankee tool.

In analyzing the events of the years between 1963 and 1966 (the coup against Bosch, the intervention, and the subsequent electoral victory of Balaguer over Bosch), it is pertinent to recall the AFL-CIO activity during that time. In 1963 AFL-CIO people, principally Andrew McLellan, the AFL-CIO Latin American representative, and Fred Somerford, United States labor attaché, were lending their assistance to those unionists interested in the overthrow of President Bosch. In the 1965 intervention the AFL-CIO supported the United States policy. In the 1966 elections the AFL-CIO strenuously opposed Bosch. The Balaguer victory was enthusiastically publicized in the June 1966 English edition of the ORIT's *Inter-American Labor Bulletin*, of which McLellan was the editor.[a] If there is one single connecting factor in these different actions during

aThis story did not appear in the Spanish edition, which according to Jáuregui is "the official edition." The English editions of the publication which was printed in Washington has been discontinued. There is now only a Spanish language publication.

the three years it is the concern with communism. McLellan and his followers felt that the Communist danger was reaching dangerous proportions in the Dominican Republic. Juan Bosch was believed by the AFL-CIO people to be naive concerning communism. For the AFL-CIO (and the ORIT local affiliated unions) Bosch's refusal to disavow Communist support (both inside and outside the labor movements) was indicative of his naïvete—and for some North American unionists, even an indication of his being controlled by the Communists.

Jáuregui's own view of the matter was that Juan Bosch was at least not wise in accepting Communist support. While respecting democratic socialist Bosch as a person the ORIT leader affirms that he could not support a man who numbered among his multiple different ideological supporters those from the CLASC and the Communist ranks.

In explaining the ORIT position, Jáuregui calls attention to the statement that ORIT issued at the time of the intervention crisis of the spring of 1965. That statement in part said:

The North American intervention provoked a psychological and doctrinal reaction which corresponds to traditional feelings of Latin America in respect to the participation of armed forces in the internal affairs of another. Such a step would have been avoided had there been prompt coordination of action by the proper inter-governmental organizations with the urgency that the situation deserved.[17]

Jáuregui would have preferred inter-American governmental action rather than a unilateral action by U.S. marines.

Jáuregui's view on this delicate matter exemplifies the problems he has had to face that are inherent in his being leader of an inter-American organization. He insists that his position was an honest one, that he and the ORIT took the best stand when all the circumstances are remembered. ORIT refused to join with the Communists and the CLASC in the 1965 crises, and in the 1966 elections in supporting the pro-Bosch forces. But within the ORIT there was also some criticism of the intervention, although its Dominican affiliate and the AFL-CIO defended it. Jáuregui further asserts that he was never anti-Bosch in a personal sense. Bosch he regarded as a likable well-intentioned professor who during his previous administration had really not paid too much attention to labor's interests. Unfortunately, according to Jáuregui, Bosch also was naive concerning the Communists.

As the ORIT leader sees it, during the 1965 crises there was a good chance that extremists from either the political right or left might have taken power. The United States intervention, while it justifiably aroused indignation throughout Latin America and could have been avoided, was he believes, understandable given the dangers the crisis posed. The threat of Communist subversion in particular, Jáuregui believes, was greater than was realized by many people. In a terribly confused and controversial matter the ORIT's neutral stance in 1965 and its nonsupport of Bosch in the 1966 election was, according to the ORIT leader, making the best of a bad situation. Jáuregui, incidentally, emphasized that the freedom of action that prevails within the ORIT was again demonstrated in 1965. As the Canadian affiliate had criticized the "Bay of Pigs" attack in 1961, so ORIT's important Peruvian affiliate, the CTV, refused to accept the majority view of ORIT in the Dominican crisis.

The ORIT press release of September 26, 1965, Jáuregui believes, clearly asserted the basic attitude of himself and his organization relative to the whole question of U.S. intervention. It reads as follows:

The Inter-American Regional Organization of Workers (ORIT) views with surprise and alarm, along with democratic public opinion in Latin America, the recent Resolution passed by the U.S. House of Representatives in which it declares that the U.S. would unilaterally impose its armed forces in Latin America if an emergency should arise by communist insurrection, said Arturo Jáuregui, ORIT Secretary General.

Although we recognize that this Resolution does not constitute a foreign policy program for the United States, [continued Jáuregui] knowing the considerable influence the House of Representatives has upon U.S. foreign policy leads us to suspect that dangerous prospects can derive from the Resolution. We cannot overlook that this Resolution cites the Monroe Doctrine as authority, despite the fact that on repeated occasions the governments of Latin America have made known their belief that the Monroe Doctrine lacks validity as an Inter-American norm.

ORIT considers it timely to reiterate that from our earliest days we have fought for the establishment of norms through which the peoples of our hemisphere could live peacefully among each other, thereby erasing the bitterness and misunderstandings which once stemmed from older policies of the United States toward Latin America.

We believe that the only sources of a juridical Inter-American system are the Charter of the United Nations, the Constituent Charter of the Organization of American States (OAS) and fundamentally, the Inter-American Treaty of Río de Janeiro (Mutual Assistance) that were signed and ratified by all the congresses and constitutional regimes of Latin America.

It cannot be denied that Latin America faces an explosive situation of terrorism and subversion of a totalitarian and imperialistic nature, fomented by the Soviet Union, Red China, and the ruthless Cuban regime. Faced with this criminal intent, we must oppose it by strict adherence to Inter-American accords and treaties and by strengthening democratic and freely elected regimes. The latter is the only and exclusive source of popular and national sovereignty. There must be no attempt in the name of communist agitation, to implement extra-legal measures that would only weaken national sovereignty. To disregard the principles of "No Intervention" in the internal affairs of each country—a principle which each country has freely subscribed to follow—or to imply a "tutelage" of the United States over the free national institutions of other countries constitutes a danger. It does not contribute towards the solving of the fundamental economic, social, cultural, and political problems for whose solution all democratic peoples are fighting, particularly the free trade unions.

We are confident that this Resolution of the U.S. House of Representatives will have no practical application nor validity and that the government of the United States will again reiterate its adhesion to Inter-American principles of friendship, harmony and concord among the peoples of Latin America. These are the principles of the Alliance for Progress.

Emilio Máspero's attitude toward U.S. intervention is less complicated for he heads a purely Latin American labor organization. Whatever calculations enter into his maintaining the more common anti-Yankee posture before his small organizations and the general *latino* public, he has been eternally vigilant in opposing any action in Latin America that reflects the cold war. He is one who stands for the Third World view. He is flatly opposed to U.S. intervention in any shape or form.

Before turning to Máspero's reaction to the two specific instances of U.S. intervention under consideration here, let us recall his views on U.S. foreign policy toward Latin America in general. The CLAT leader believes that both capitalism and communism are each to be opposed but that capitalist United States poses, at this time, the greater danger to Latin America. In accordance with this belief, Máspero, while criticizing the United States and Russian policies affecting Latin America, directs his major fire against the United States. For him a dangerous U.S. complex of forces is at work in Latin America: the Department of State, the CIA, the Pentagon—and the AFL-CIO foreign policy hierarchy. The State Department protects American business interests and pursues an irrational policy with regard to communism, with which it appears to be eternally concerned, to the exclusion of more important matters. The CIA continually pursues its espionage seeking to infiltrate its agents into a wide variety of governmental and important nongovernmental corporate groups.[18] The Pentagon supplies Latin American militarists with arms, inflates their egos, and aids various preferred dictators. It stands at the ready to intervene when the U.S. president, for whatever reason (often on advice from Pentagon people and/or CIA and Department of State intelligence officers), decides that the security or welfare of the United States necessitates the intervention. As Máspero sees it the AFL-CIO, cooperating with the CIA, advises the State Department, where it does not merely carry out State Department policies. On its own, the AFL-CIO pursues a vigorous policy of intervention in native union affairs and local politics, again largely motivated by the desire of cold war zealots to check presumed Communist efforts to infiltrate local unions or subvert local governments.

Máspero believes that if the North American public knew all this it would disavow its government's policies. These policies in Latin America, especially as they have been reflected in the events which have taken place since Lyndon Johnson succeeded John Kennedy to the presidency, are the CLASC leader's main target. He bluntly attacked what he called the U.S. "invasion" of the Dominican Republic as well as the earlier "Bay of Pigs" adventure in Cuba. His bitter criticism of U.S. intervention against Castro's Cuba and the Dominican Republic are consistent with his analyses of general U.S. policies in Latin America.[19]

Opposed himself to Castro's communism at home and to earlier Fidelista actions throughout Latin America, Máspero has been sharply critical of the U.S. policy towards Cuba. An avowed social revolutionary, he takes the position that the United States has largely supported those Cuban and Latin American reactionaries who use the specter of Castro's tyranny to frighten people into turning to counterrevolutionaries of a conservative or rightist bent to crush necessary social revolutions. He views the AFL-CIO's support of U.S. intervention in Cuba (and the Dominican Republic) in this light.

To Máspero the American trade union leadership in siding with the pro-Batista *Confederación de Trabajadores Cubanos* (CTC), the ORIT affiliate, in the years immediately prior to the Castro successful revolution, and later in blessing the "Bay of Pigs" landing, reflects the reactionary role of the whole U.S. policy of intervention in Cuba. Piously proclaiming that, as they were originally anti-Batista, they are now anti-Castro, the AFL-CIO interventionists sought and continue to seek to use the troubled Cuban scene for pro-Yankee, antisocial revolutionary ends. In this the ORIT, he declares, must share the blame for following its American masters in the ranks of labor and (via the AFL-CIO) in the Department of State.[20]

To sum up: Máspero supported the Castro revolution in the early years as a needed revolution in freedom, as an indigenous Latin American revolution which should be kept out of the cold war conflict. This position was later reiterated by the CLASC in 1964 in its seminars of solidarity with the people and workers of Cuba. By the time of Castro's Tricontinental Conference of Havana in 1966, however, it had become obvious to the CLASC leader that Cuba under Castro had moved into the orbit of the cold war. Cuba, for Máspero, had become the main center in Latin America of outside intervening imperialistic forces—both capitalist imperialism and Communist imperialism—represented by the United States and the Soviet Union respectively.

Capitalist imperialist efforts to reenter Cuba was successfully thrown back at the Bay of Pigs and Fidel Castro, according to Máspero, has liberated Cuba from the U.S. meddling in Cuban affairs which had plagued its history. For doing this Máspero believes that the Cuban leader deserves commendation, not only for freeing Cuba but for pointing the way to all of Latin America, which has suffered from the historic policy of U.S. interference and, on occasion, outright military intervention. Castro, nevertheless, in Máspero's view, is unfortunately a dictator who has permitted the imperialistic policy of international communism to thrust itself into Cuba and Latin America.

Máspero, then, is critical of *yanqui* imperialism wherever it appears—in Latin America or elsewhere. But in criticizing what he calls actions of U.S. agression he does not fail to also denounce similar Soviet aggression. Just as he denounced the American actions in the Dominican Republic in the spring of 1965, so he bitterly criticized the invasion of Czechoslovakia by the armed forces of the Warsaw Pact nations led by the USSR in the summer of 1968. He made it plain that he disagreed with the Latin American parties, the pro-Soviet trade unions in the WFTU, and all Communists and their sympathizers who defended the invasion of Czechoslovakia. In "The WCL Seen From Latin America" (the special edition of *Labor*, Numbers 2-4, 1970 published in Brussels by the WCL as, *The WCL: Unity in Diversity*, on pp. 22-23), he writes:

The American landing in Santo Domingo in 1965 and the invasion of Czechoslovakia . . . in 1968 provided the Latin American workers with further illustrations of the deep crisis currently running through the international labor movement. The majority of the pro-American trade union organizations affiliated with the ICFTU, and especially the Latin-American organizations depending on the American Institute for the Development of Free Trade Unionism, supported the third occupation of the Dominican Republic by the marines of the North American empire. For their part most of the pro-Soviet trade union organization of the WTCU and in particular those closely linked with the Latin American communist parties . . . gave their backing to the occupation of Czechoslovakia by the troops and allies of the Soviet empire.

It should thus be no problem for the reader to understand Máspero's more detailed view of the United States intervention in the Dominican Republic in April 1965. To him it was an invasion to thwart a native national movement which aspired to building a better social order. What he regards as the same old bogeyman of a Communist takeover was trotted out by the U.S. government and its AFL-CIO supporters and advisors, to hide the truth and pressure Latin American countries into acting as part of the open conspiracy against the progressive forces in the Dominican Republic. Once again, the cold war strategy was invoked to victimize Latin American patriots. But let Máspero speak for himself:

. . . I believe that the case of the Dominican Republic is a warning for all Latin Americans. I have just come from there. I talked with Colonel Camaño, with labor leaders and politicians of that country and I can affirm that the Yankees have stopped an authentic national revolution cold. Everything that they are seeking to make the public opinion of the continent believe concerning the Dominican crisis is false. I roundly deny to anyone who may say that the communists directed that revolution, they never had control of it. [And again:] . . . (The) United States and many other countries of Latin America frustrated a national revolution. It is not to be thought of as strange if the Americans picked out the Dominican Republic as the stage upon which to achieve what they sought: the creation of the Inter-American Peace Force to justify new interventions in happenings that soon enough will move the hemisphere. Such as the cases of Guatemala and Colombia. Thusly, Latin America legalizes a way through which the Americans will be enabled to continue to deform continent demands and needs today.[21]

The later attitude of the United States, of the AFL-CIO and of ORIT's affiliate in the Dominican Republic during the 1966 elections held in an atmosphere of fear, in which Juan Bosch was defeated, from Máspero's point of view, only served to underline the truth of his perceptions. To him the successful Balaguer obviously was the candidate of the oligarchy, the Church, and the military. To him his position and that of the CLASC during the civil strife and its aftermath was an honorable one that championed *latino* interests and those of the masses who desired long-needed reforms and social democracy. He, the CLASC, and its affilitate in the Dominican Republic, CASC, had stood against the intervening *coloso*, against a glaring breach of the pledge of nonintervention. He and the CLASC had supported a progressive native cause during and after the intervention. To him Jáuregui and the ORIT, caught up in their connections with the AFL-CIO and the ORIT's Dominican affiliate, the CONATRAL, in contrast, had opposed Juan Bosch and social democracy and aided the local reactionaries.

Máspero is satisfied that the workers of the Dominican Republic subsequently indicated their agreement with him by making the CLASC affiliate in their country the major trade union confederation. The Autonomous Confederation of Christian Trade Unionists (CASC) which had been challenging the ORIT affiliate, the National Confederation of Workers (CONATRAL), did move ahead of its ORIT rival as a consequence of the hostilities. It is ironic that one of the few strong affiliating labor conferations in CLASC that successfully challenged the ORIT in the Dominican Republic should in some respects owe its position to the U.S. decision to intervene in the Dominican Republic.

The O.A.S.

The Dominican intervention also is of consequence in another matter which illustrates the differing attitudes of Máspero and Jáuregui, namely, their views of the Organization of American States (the OAS) and of cooperation with this inter-American agency. The OAS Charter, drawn up in Bogotá in 1948, contains the famous Article 15 which forbids any state or groups of states the right "to intervene directly or indirectly for any reason whatever in the internal or external affairs of any other state." At the same time the troublesome matter of how to act to protect human rights and democratic interests without any nation resorting to intervention was presumed to be taken care of by Article 19. This reads that "measures adopted for the maintenance of peace and security in accordance with existing treaties do not constitute a violation of the principles set forth in Article 15. . . ."[22]

The OAS in addition to being concerned with intervention, the adjustment of differences in avoiding war in the Western Hemisphere, also seeks to promote common action in the economic, social, and cultural development of its members. In carrying out these latter duties the OAS has since 1962 endeavored to assist labor throughout Latin America. For example, two inter-American conferences at the ministry level, in May 1963 and in May 1966, were sponsored by the OAS. As a result of these conferences the Trade Union Technical Advisory Committee (COSATE) in 1964, and the Permanent Technical Committee on Labor Matters (COTPAL) in 1966, were established within the OAS. Technical assistance is provided to the trade unions by COSATE and to the governmental ministers by COTPAL.

Máspero has always been leery of the OAS, seeing it principally as a kind of pious pontificator rationalizing the interests of the United States and its Latin American conservative collaborators. OAS action following the crisis of the U.S. intervention in the Dominican Republic in 1965 was to Máspero just one more glaring example in a series of how the OAS for years excused U.S. aggression or cooperated in supporting U.S. interests. With the OAS composed of a number of weak powers and one superpower, the "Chickens-Fox" analogy is a most apt one. The United States, Máspero believes, has repeatedly acted on its own behind the façade of the OAS, using its great power in various ways to accomplish its purposes. To return to the Dominican case, the United States first violated the OAS charter by the unilateral action. Then soon came a so-called "joint" military action, when OAS forces arrived later. This "cooperative" action, the first of its kind in hemispheric history was the precedent leading to the creation of a permanent Inter-American Peace Force. Máspero's feelings, specifically with regard to the Dominican intervention, was expressed dramatically in May 1965 when CLASC's representatives walked out of the Caracas meeting of COSATE when they were refused permission to read a political statement expressing the CLASC view of the OAS position in the Dominican crisis.

Specifically as concerns labor and OAS, Máspero has expressed criticism as regards the 1963 meeting of Latin American labor ministers in Bogotá. Máspero charged that originally the ORIT with its powerful AFL-CIO membership was the only trade union organization invited by the OAS to this conference of labor ministers. "Only after the CLASC mobilized all its strength throughout Latin America were our delegates invited."[23]

While deeply suspicious of the OAS Máspero has not entirely broken with it. After a lengthy period of boycotting COSATE he succeeded in renewing CLASC's participation in that Committee.[24] But he has never regarded OAS as an agency of true inter-American cooperation.

Jáuregui has from the beginning held the generally favorable view of that agency as an instrument of inter-American cooperation. During his regime he has encouraged the participation of frequently outspoken OAS labor specialists at innumerable ORIT sponsored conventions, conferences, and educational seminars at the regional and national levels. He has also impressed upon the OAS the desire for greater trade union participation in the decision-shaping circles of the Alliance for Progress. The OAS some years ago began to emphasize the roles of the labor ministries of the different member countries, but for Jáuregui this was not enough. He has pressed for the right of labor union officials to have a more influential voice in the ministries since he believes that in too many Latin American countries labor's interests are neglected. It is significant that the Fifth ORIT Congress (Rio de Janeiro, 1961) which elected him as full-fledged secretary general was the one that originated ORIT's now familiar role of emphasizing labor's participation in national planning agencies.

As for the former CLASC's relations with OAS Jáuregui takes the position that the CLASC revealed itself as an agency for inter-American disruption rather than cooperation. This, he says was indicated repeatedly by CLASC's cooperation with the Communists and by its very negative actions toward the OAS itself. Believing that Máspero and company have through their actions left no doubt as to their negative and obstructive stance concerning the ideals and purposes of the OAS, Jáuregui and his organization bitterly objected to what they viewed as the lenient attitude of the secretary general in permitting CLASC to renew its participation in COSATE. A resolution of the ORIT Executive Council in 1968, which was sent to the OAS, illustrated this feeling. It indicated that the ORIT was not disposed to participate in any meetings as long as the CLASC (which did not according to the ORIT represent the Latin American workers) continued its negative posture. The resolution went on to assert that if in spite of this warning the CLASC continued its obstructive policies then the ORIT would be obliged to have its affiliates refuse participation in any future conferences, meetings, commissions, etc., of the OAS in which CLASC participated.[25]

So much for an indication of the rivals views towards the OAS. The fundamentally conflicting views that Máspero and Jáuregui maintain relative to the whole matter of the value of Pan-Americanism or inter-Americanism itself make their respective attitudes towards the OAS not too difficult to understand.

5 Conflicting Perspectives III: Trade Unions and the Political System

The rivalry examined here reveals two avowedly democratic labor leaders in bitter conflict. Each takes a basically different road in accomplishing his task, which to each is that of strengthening Latin American labor. Jáuregui views himself as the pragmatist—his stated goals, which he calls revolutionary, do not demand for their achievement extreme changes. His methods are those which follow the accepted rules of the way the political game is played in Latin America by various contenders who have displayed possession of power capabilities. Working within the system Jáuregui, the long-time *Aprista*, continues the ORIT closeness to populism and support of the various populist parties. While he is interested in the improvement of Latin American society, his principal interest is in developing and strengthening democratic trade unionism.

Máspero is more extreme in goals, methods, and in the scope of the end he envisions. He militantly advocates social revolution, flatly opposing capitalism and openly proclaiming his advocacy of socialist communitarianism. Unlike Jáuregui there is in Máspero a definite note of pessimism towards the existing institutions in Latin America. Where CLASC (now CLAT) has supported political parties these have been of Christian democratic persuasion. However, it has been the left-wing and/or *rebelde* elements of Christian democracy's parties that find favor with Máspero. The CLAT is at present best described as having an eclectic position as far as outright support of political parties is concerned. A radical revolutionary non-Marxist movement, it finds in today's Latin America no extant political party with which it is in accord. Certainly (in contrast to the ORIT) it disavows populism and the populist parties. It is a movement that its leader has pushed beyond the moderate aim of advancing trade union democracy towards the vision of achieving a new social order.

Jáuregui's Stance

Jáuregui's approach is that which sees labor increasingly accepted as an important interest group by the other corporate groups—military, church, landowners—which mobilize power in Latin American politics. The ORIT leader is impressed by the advances organized labor has made in Latin America since World War I. He likes to remind his critics of the depressed conditions in which the labor movement had its origins, and of the obstacles overcome in making headway in the harsh ambient. These accomplishments mean to him that in most countries a leader may work within the system to eventually rise above it.

Working within the system means working closely with national unions that have achieved governmental and social approval such as the CTM of Mexico, the CTV of Venezuela and the Peruvian CTP. Jáuregui believes that the officially approved labor movements should be used whenever possible for they are the ones most likely to succeed in strengthening the ORIT in their particular countries. So although some may leave much to be desired with regard to democratic processes, he will cooperate with them. While recently under his direction the ORIT has turned to working with those who are organizing in the countryside, the majority of ORIT's Latin affiliates are from the older urban type unions that for some time have been accepted by government and employers.

Jáuregui knows very well the criticisms that are made of some of these affiliates of the ORIT—that they are principally the agencies of political parties and the governments, that they are corrupt and run by self-serving labor *caudillos*. He flatly rejects these criticisms, particularly when they come from those like CLAT officials whom, he says, only mean harm to the ORIT. To others who raise such questions he observes that the criticisms are exaggerated, that he as well as his rivals or any labor officials operate in an imperfect world and that these affiliates, the established labor confederations, are important and useful in helping to strengthen labor's position in a very difficult everyday real world.

All things considered Jáuregui believes there has been a miraculous accomplishment in the development of more responsible trade unionism in Latin America. He agrees that there is much more to be done to make labor throughout Latin America an important political force and to improve the miserable conditions of the workers' lives. He believes that working within the system, with all its frustrations, complexities, and even dangers, is the best way of achieving that better future. He relies a great deal upon workers' education and other less specialized techniques to develop the younger Latin American potential democratic leaders who will more and more in the future replace the present labor *caudillos* and *caciques* whom, to repeat, he does not scorn. His party politics is that of the middle-class populist variety which has also been the politics of most Latin American labor leaders since the rise of these parties in the years between the two world wars. It is a politics with an indigenous strain challenging the oligarchy, seeking to bring about fundamental changes by means of the classical operation of politics in an area in which democracy is but one accepted alternative road to power.

A major continuing problem for Jáuregui has, of course, been the one related to the AFL-CIO affiliates of the ORIT. This matter of the powerful *yanquis* allied with weaker *latinos* within one organization has been with every secretary general since the ORIT was founded.

Given the image of *el coloso del norte* that has long been held by the majority of Latin Americans who affect public opinion, as well as by other critics of U.S. foreign policy and that of the AFL-CIO complex, Jáuregui's North American ties give him and the ORIT a highly questionable appearance. To such critics the ORIT is a transmission agency of the U.S. government and particularly of U.S. labor decision makers who work hand-in-glove with the government. Controlled by the Americans its main function has been seen as fighting communism.

Jáuregui's and the ORIT's admittedly friendly relations to the Americans are well known. What is not widely appreciated are the ORIT's disagreements with the AFL-CIO and AIFLD. These differences "within the family" have been several and continuing.

To begin with Jáuregui feels that although AFL-CIO policies established in its conventions which relate to the ORIT are always firmly supportive, serious problems arise in the implementation of those policies. In this regard Jáuregui is critical of the AFL-CIO's office of Inter-American Affairs, and particularly of its director, Andrew McLelland. Jáuregui believes that it is a great pity that the powerful, well-meaning AFL-CIO does not have a top executive in charge of Latin American affairs. In his opinion, because of this lack the AFL-CIO deals with Latin America largely, to quote him, "by inertia." McLelland, according to Jáuregui, has over the years disparaged the role of the ORIT while at the same time attempting to force it into actions which Jáuregui opposed. At times, in his continuing all-out attacks against Marxists and his too sweeping accusations, McLelland's extremism leads to embarrassing situations. Such was the case in the Dominican Republic in relation to Juan Bosch. Again, with the election of Salvador Allende to the Chilean presidency, McLelland, according to the ORIT general secretary, urged a definite ORIT stand in opposition to Allende. Jáuregui, while disagreeing with Marxist Allende, takes the position that Allende is the democratically elected president of Chile. As such, as long as Allende follows constitutional practices, he is the legitimate head of a Latin American state. Accordingly, as has been his custom in all such cases as a courteous formality, Jáuregui sent the newly elected president of Chile a telegram of congratulations from ORIT in the fall of 1970. There have been several other disagreements between Jáuregui and the director of the AFL-CIO's Latin American section. In the great bureaucracy of the AFL-CIO with its internal conflicts and dissents and with its different policy executors always seeking the ear of President George Meany, the whole situation can affect adversely AFL-CIO's relation with the ORIT. The root of the matter in Jáuregui's opinion lies with the inadequate and indeed obstructive executive leadership in the powerful American labor body's office dealing with Latin American affairs.[1]

The American Institute for Free Labor Development and its relationship to ORIT is a particular subject for Jáuregui critics. Again, while the firm friend of the AIFLD, Jáuregui in rejecting the criticism asserts that his posture with regard to the AIFLD, as in the case of the AFL-CIO, indicates his true position. This, to repeat once again, is that of "friend, but no colonial." Since the charges that it is largely through the AIFLD that the Americans exercise their controls in the field over the ORIT it is worth explaining in some detail the ORIT leader's view of what he feels constitute evidence of the truth of his position in this matter.

The AIFLD to Jáuregui is an agency largely supported by the United States government. In this it is like similar agencies from other countries with an interest in Latin America, such as the rival *stifdungen* of West Germany, with which the ORIT and the CLAT cooperate. Many countries have such agencies with a special interest in labor in Latin America. The CLASC (now the CLAT) enjoys the support of the Konrad Adenauer *stifdung*, the one of Christian Democratic support from West Germany. The Friedrich Ebert *stifdung* of the German Social Democrats has worked with the ORIT. All of these particular agencies assist Latin American labor organizations from time to time. The AIFLD does not financially support the ORIT. It has greatly helped the ORIT in its workers educational programs, and in various special seminars and programs that have been held in the ORIT school in Cuernavaca. Of course, the AIFLD pays its share of the costs of these programs. And it has been the principal cooperator in them—cooperating along with representatives from other countries' various agencies as well as those from the U.S., and the OAS.

The relationship of AIFLD and the ORIT is a special and naturally close one since AIFLD is the AFL-CIO's main field operation spread throughout Latin America. Arturo Jáuregui is an ex officio member of the AIFLD. He approves of the AIFLD and welcomes its assistance. But, once again, he insists that his approval for the AIFLD is because its work is basically helpful to Latin American labor. He feels that the Institute has done a significant job in promoting housing, cooperatives, workers' banks, workers' education, and—in general—has been helpful in promoting the philosophy of free trade unionism.

In the interests of Latin American labor, and of the ORIT, itself, Jáuregui has certain criticisms concerning AIFLD operations. These criticisms center around the AIFLD's country program directors. He feels that very often the Institute has sent to Latin America as country program directors persons who lack a knowledge of the sensibilities of the people in the area. Some of these country program directors, he says, act as paternalistic commissars. Some have no trade union background. They are bright academics, Ph.D.'s in labor relations and sociology, but with little or no practical trade union experience. And some of them have been what Jáuregui calls "politicians."

In some cases AIFLD country program directors, in the view of the ORIT leader, have been more interested in building contacts with embassies (particularly those representing the United States), universities, and even with employers, than in identifying themselves with the unions. Some of them, moreover, have been decidedly deficient in their knowledge of the Spanish or Portuguese languages. With regard to contacts with U.S. embassies some of the country program directors have acted as if they, and not the embassy labor attaché, were to all intents and purposes the real labor attaché from the United States. This has occurred even when, according to Jáuregui, the labor attaché of the embassy has repeatedly demonstrated a more comprehensive understanding of labor and trade union problems in the particular country than have these "un-official" labor attachés.

Depending upon the maturity and strength of the central labor confederation of the particular country the AIFLD's country program directors degree of control of the workers' educational program of that country will vary. Where the native central confederation is administered by *latinos* of independence and resourcefulness the relationship, in Jáuregui's view, has been very good. Where the native leadership is lacking in resourcefulness the AIFLD programs have been, he says, too paternalistic and too *yanqui*.

Jáuregui agrees that the country program directors must have a degree of autonomy in their relationships with the central office in Washington. But he believes that at times the central office has given too much respect for the autonomy of some of its country program directors. He is particularly critical of the central office failure to stop the controversies that at times have been originated by certain country program directors with the ORIT. And here again, as in the whole matter of what he regards as the good intentions of the AIFLD to work positively with the ORIT, the pressures that are put upon it in various ways by the critics of the ORIT and of Jáuregui within the AFL-CIO bureaucracy, unfortunately do exist to damage the good work of the Institute. As already indicated it is the Inter-American Office of the AFL-CIO that Jáuregui has felt particularly unhappy about in this regard.[2]

For Jáuregui his actions towards his allies of the AFL-CIO and the AIFLD are proof that neither he nor the ORIT are the puppets of the *yanquis* as his opponents charge. He is emphatic in his denials that the ORIT is financially supported by either the AFL-CIO or the AIFLD. The AFL-CIO he says has paid its assessments in the past, when it was a member of the ICFTU, to the International Solidarity Fund from which the ORIT then (as now) does draw support. The AFL-CIO as a member of the ORIT pays its proportionate assessment, as any other affiliate. The major American labor confederation has contributed in many ways to the building of the ORIT school in Cuernavaca. But so have important American trade union organizations that are not members of the AFL-CIO. So has the central labor confederation of Canada, the Canadian Labor Congress, whom the CLAT also accuses of thus helping *yanqui* imperialism. And finally, so has the CTM. It was through the powerful Mexican affiliate's efforts that the governor of the state of Morelos donated the land in Cuernavaca upon which the ORIT school was built. Thus the different affiliates have contributed to the building of the ORIT school. The AIFLD has paid its assessments of the costs of programs in which it has participated in the operation of the school and its special programs, but this Jáuregui insists does not make the ORIT the financial dependency of the AIFLD.

Jáuregui wonders exactly where all ORIT's various critics get their information since not a single one of them, including American academics and liberal magazine writers, according to the ORIT leader, have ever conducted any investigations that he knows of either at the ORIT headquarters in Mexico City or at the ORIT Institute (the labor college) at Cuernavaca.[3]

Having presented these differences and other related matters which to Jáuregui constitute proof positive of his independence we must remind ourselves that the ORIT leader is proud to be allied with the AFL-CIO and the AIFLD in what he regards as a mutually beneficial relationship of inter-American cooperation. He welcomes the technical and financial assistance that the more affluent and experienced American trade unions can contribute to the development of a viable, free, Latin American labor movement. He is happy that the more experienced and affluent North Americans (including Canadians) are so willing to assist their less experienced and less fortunate brothers in Latin America. He is of a group of *latinos* who were opposing communism before the ORIT was founded. He and these others were happy to join the Yankees in the founding of the ORIT, and in its inveterate campaigns against what all viewed as the threat of communism to the Latin American labor movement. AFL-CIO and/or AIFLD postures and activities concerning communism or its dangers, such as in the cases referred to in this study, in Cuba, the Dominican Republic and Brazil, have received a sympathetic understanding from Jáuregui even where in some details it might be said that he privately disagreed. And more evidence could be cited of the cooperative policy, but none of this, Jáuregui insists, in any way gives credence to the views held by his opponents that the ORIT is the mouthpiece of George Meany, AFL-CIO president, or of Jay Lovestove, the architect of the AFL-CIO foreign policy with its extreme concern with the Communist danger.[4] ORIT, *qua* ORIT, on the matters referred to here as well as others, has issued its own position in separate statements. While in overall effect these may agree with the positions of the Americans, they do not approve of, or justify, all AFL-CIO and AIFLD actions. And the affiliates of the ORIT who have objected to the majority position have had their objections noted.

For many years the ORIT paid little attention to the matter of constructing a carefully built guiding and supporting message of inspiration for its members. It may be Jáuregui's pride in being concerned with practical realities and accomplishments, or that the nature of the ORIT itself worked against any serious effort in building an official distinctive trade union ideology that accounts for this. Whatever the reason this lack of genuine concern until recently with the importance of ideology has been a distinctive difference on the part of the ORIT leader in comparison with his rival, Emilio Máspero. "The Philosophy of the ORIT" as we have seen was a very general statement of the purpose of *latinos* joining with *yanquis* to work together in a common cause of building and strengthening free trade unionism in the Western Hemisphere. Communism and specifically Fidelista communism are singled out for particular mention as the example of the chief dangers arising to free labor from totalitarianism and militarism which the ORIT opposes in any form. Working together in inter-American cooperation *latinos* and North Americans will seek to achieve social democracy by combining political democracy with economic democracy. In the fight against economic imperialism the trade unions of the United States as allies of the ORIT receive special mention. Presidents Kennedy and Johnson are saluted for their efforts in constructing and sustaining the new friendly United States policy towards Latin America.

All in all "The Philosophy" represents a broad, eclectic statement which was the reflection of older trade union groupings of established labor bodies within their societies. Recently ideology has, as indicated, been of increasing concern to Jáuregui. Yet because of the nature of the ORIT—not only in the comparative conservativism of its affiliates, but in the autonomy of each affiliate which is characteristic of the ORIT—an electism is bound to continue. This would appear so even if the more militant and radical views expressed by some delegates in the Cuernavaca discussions of January 1971 make an impact in any future formal ideological statement.[a] When to this is added the aversion that the present ORIT secretary general has to "declamations from balconies" (his reference to Máspero's ideological oratory) there appears small chance that the ORIT ideology will ever be marked by a single-voiced fervent missionary appeal.

Máspero's Stance

Jáuregui's rival burns with a different light. Emilio Máspero does not expect too much to result from working within the established avenues of the political system. To be sure he and his movement have never had much attraction for the older and more established labor bodies, nor for that matter the vast majority of viable labor unions in Latin America. But Máspero has always indicated his lack of faith in the effectiveness of the political institutions in Latin America for meaningful change. His direction from the time of his entrance into the CLASC was away from the moderate practices advocated by the early leaders such as José Goldsack. Máspero's bent has been steadily away from the moderate path towards what CLAT stands for today, which can be described as a radical non-Marxist, humanistic socialism. With the reincarnation of CLASC into CLAT the Máspero push to make the former Christian trade union movement go beyond organizing trade unions and become a revolutionary instrument of all the workers for creating a new social order becomes evident. To be sure Máspero

---

[a]The complexity of the whole question of a coherent unified ORIT ideology is illustrated when it is recalled that among those in the Cuernavaca discussions who criticized capitalism along with communism, the United States along with Russia, who favored some kind of socialism, who called upon the ORIT to construct a militant revolutionary ideology—among all these were some of the most outspoken critics of Christian socialism and of the CLASC.

has encouraged trade union organization and actively aided the various activities, formal and informal, concerned with workers' education. He has also actively supported Christian Democratic political parties. But his heart is set on the "big plan"—the gaining of the socialist communitarian society which will replace the present highly unsatisfactory social order.

All of this gives to the organization Máspero heads the distinct favor of militancy and revolution. CLAT is an avowed workers' revolutionary body. It will seek to peacefully attain its aims. It will, as indicated, use whatever political institutions it feels aid in its quest, but it is prepared for violence that may arise from a policy of supporting revolution "in all its consequences." And it is decidedly pessimistic about the overall value of the political party system in Latin America. Specifically, it has lost all faith in populism and the populist parties.

Máspero's view of populism constitutes another sharp difference with Jáuregui. The ORIT leader, who still professes the faith of the *Apristas*, sees populism as a progressive middle-class ideology with a concern for the welfare of the labor movement. Like other *latinos* Jáuregui feels that all things considered the populist program has helped to advance the social welfare in those countries where the populist political parties have been active. While Jáuregui, unlike Máspero, has not manifested his beliefs concerning populism in any extended writings, his informal conversations and his support of the so-called populist parties in various Latin American countries, a support also which has been expressed by the ORIT, are indicative of his view. On the other hand, to Máspero the so-called populist revolutions represent a deceit and a farce which have ensnared the people and obstructed the workers movement.

The CLAT leader examines populism in some detail. He notes it as an original political eruption of the people and of vast sections of the working class. Populism he says, aroused the hopes and stimulated the aspirations of the people. In fact it is the last card of imperialist capitalism. It seeks to obstruct the potential emerging popular revolution and to integrate the people into the neo-capitalist order. Populism's surface reforms restrict the building of a true working-class consciousness. Populism really manipulates the workers in order to gain, regain, or retain power, without there being any basic change in the present social order. It seeks to despoil the working class, to rob it of its historic mission to fight for a new social order. It is sufficient, Máspero concludes, to observe the many specific helps that the U.S. Department of State and the big corporations of its empire have given to Latin American populism.[5]

Máspero must, like Jáuregui, bear the burden of being labeled the tool of outside foreign interests. His opponents charge that he is generously supported by European sources, Catholic Church-sponsored private bodies, the Church hierarchy of West Germany, and the coffers of the WCL. While this charge may not be as harmful to him and his organization in an area like Latin America as that of being linked with *los yanquis* which Jáuregui has to bear, it is not something that can be taken lightly. In recent years, especially, Latin Americans have become particularly sensitive to accusations of outside dependency. Answering these accusations of foreign influence Máspero, like Jáuregui in similar circumstances, flatly denies them. Any funding from abroad he says is legitimate in its nature and is not indicative of foreign control. While he enjoys the support of the WCL leadership and those important European institutions inside and outside church and governments who believe in the WCL philosophy, he is no tool, but an independent revolutionary labor leader. He has been criticized by moderates within the same circles not only for his militant position in Latin America but for the same militant stance when participating in European and world councils of the WCL. To some, even among the majority who support him, he is a very troublesome and a very opinionated and charismatic figure. Members of the majority view who aid him have commented on his irritating ways, but they are convinced that he is the leader to support in Latin America. That decision was made some years ago when the fiery Máspero successfully challenged the leadership of the moderate Goldsack.

Much more serious is another accusation by Máspero's critics. This is the one that he and his organization are "confessionals" that they are really the labor allies of the Catholic Church. This is indeed a serious accusation made in a part of the world where organized labor and much of society although nominally Catholic has traditionally been anti-clerical, and anti-Church.[6]

Throughout the years of the CLASC Máspero was bedeviled by the "confessional" charge associated with the name of his organization. To these charges Máspero in effect replied when he dealt with the meaning of the Christian nature of his confederation. This Christian nature referred strictly to a type of humanism emanating from Christianity, but which any worker, Christian or not, could accept. During his many years in CLASC he has many times criticized that part of the Catholic Church's historic record sustaining an exploitative social order in Latin America. During that time, also, he expressed his willingness to cooperate tactically at times with all forces, including Marxists of different persuasions, where such cooperation was deemed helpful to the workers in the long run. These same actions in even more extreme form have characterized Máspero's position in the transformation of CLASC to CLAT. Now the Latin American labor movement which he leads, like the world body in Brussels to which it is affiliated, no longer carries the word "Christian" in its title. Now, as we have seen, as the CLAT it is even more leery of any possibilities direct or indirect of Church control; thus the repeated warnings against Church paternalism. Accepting the support of religions, when that is freely given, Máspero warns against the intrusion of clericalism in any form into the labor movement.

In the light of this Máspero might demand from his critics how it is possible that he could be conceived of being in any way "confessional" or leading a "confessional" organization: He who has criticized the historic role of religion in seeking to develop among the workers an attitude of passivity and resignation in the face of the miseries of their existence? He who argues that today religion is being called upon to legitimize the modern development of capitalism into the continuing exploitative neo-capitalism? He who has gone to great extremes in warning of the dangers from even the left-wing clergy to the autonomy and independence of the labor movement?

The contrast between Máspero and his rival relative to the factor of ideology requires further elaboration if its reality is to be fully appreciated. The differences are not only that Máspero has from the beginning been more concerned with the importance of building a workers philosophy (which he views as an universal message to all workers), and that the nature of his creed is a militant radical "missionary" one. The contrast lies also in the breadth and depth of the message that he presents to the workers as he calls upon them to fulfill their historic task.

The major indications of the breadth of the Máspero-CLAT ideology has been presented here in broad strokes. These include among others such things as a detailed examination of capitalism—including the manner in which capitalism shapes and influences social institutions, the family, education, religion—the nature of the class struggle, the criticism of communism as well as capitalism, and of Soviet imperialism along with the more immediate dangers of the imperialism of *el coloso del norte.*

As to the tendency toward depth, Máspero's treatment of the "class struggle" may serve as one example—as well as a further contrast with Jáuregui in relation to the question of ideology. It will be recalled that in discussing the nature of class struggle Máspero makes the point that for him it is a means to an end, and not an end in itself. He contrasts this view with that of the Marxists whom he asserts refused to subordinate the class struggle to moral values. Marxism, he says, by refusing to make moral values primary, by subordinating moral values to historical development, and by refuting the right of moral conscience to judge history, destroyed the autonomy of action of the workers' movement, and values which animate it and made it into a totally alienated instrument.

In his insistence on this view of the class struggle Máspero is in the tradition of those socialists who put moral purpose as the end for which they were fighting. Máspero will not allow any presumed scientific interpretation of the class struggle doctrine to usurp the superior position of idealism and high moral purpose. The Marxists insist that the class struggle is a reflection of reality—it shapes morality. Máspero separates idealism and morals from reality and argues that the moral ends are supreme. Here, of course, one finds an expression of the whole morals vs. science argument that has divided socialists at least since the days of Eduard Bernstein's revisionism which began in the 1890s.

Concluding Note

In concluding this attempt to present the contrasts involved in the contest between these rivals, mention at least should be made of their distinct personalities. In comparison to Máspero, Jáuregui is less of a charismatic figure. He appears much less tense, more of the steady labor administrator primarily concerned with trade union affairs, less suspicious of those who disagree with him although convinced of the correctness of his views. While he is a less charismatic figure than his opponent he is by no means a passive individual. Máspero is the dynamic figure, the fervent orator, the "driven" person whose interest in trade unionism is there, but who, at bottom, is more the political leader moving beyond trade unionism.

In the course of my research throughout Latin America, Europe, and the United States, in discussions concerning the two men, I found that there was more definite reaction, whether pro or con, to Máspero's personality than to that of Jáuregui. People who disliked Jáuregui would mention his stubbornness, his cleverness, his efforts (especially in the matter of various differing figures in the United States labor elite) to be all things to all men. But there was little of the vehemence that was expressed when Máspero was criticized. To the *critics*, and these included some of the moderates of the WCL circle and European lay and clerical supporters of the CLASC-CLAT movement, Máspero appears as some kind of a Frankenstein-created monster whose bluntness and aggressiveness have only compounded the dismaying result that his "politicking" has brought. As has been mentioned, even some of his European supporters do not approve of his interpersonal relations, much as they stand behind him as the best man for the times in Latin America.

6

Interpretations, Observations, Conclusions

As regional organizations of differing world labor confederations both ORIT and CLASC (now CLAT) were born in ideological conflict. From the beginning ORIT reflected the interest of the International Confederation of Free Trade Unions (ICFTU)–and particularly of its affiliate at that time, the AFL–in combatting communism among the workers in postwar Latin America. Pro-Communist views at that time were expressed in the Western Hemisphere by the Confederation of Latin American Workers, the CTAL. Founded in 1938 as an anti-fascist labor organization of liberal-left persuasion, it remained so through the years of the Second World War. For a variety of reasons, which included uneasy relationships between some of its affiliates and the basic distrust between Lombardo Toledano, its president (a Marxist but not a Communist), and the AFL which had little sympathy for it, the CTAL during the last year of the war had come under the control of Moscow-line Communists. In its metamorphosis the CTAL resembled the World Federation of Trade Unions, the international labor body to which it had become affiliated.

CLASC arrives on the scene in 1954 (some three years after the founding of the ORIT) to oppose both communism and the ORIT. In its policies it too manifested the viewpoint of a world labor grouping, the then International Federation of Christian Trade Unions (IFCTU), of which it was the Latin American affiliate. Like the IFCTU, the CLASC displayed an increasingly elastic policy in dealing with Communists. Like the IFCTU, too, it also moved more to the left in its ethic of Christian humanism. Its "parent" body, the IFCTU, following the earlier example of the important French affiliate dropped the name "Christian" from its title in 1968 and became the World Congress of Labor (WCL). The change of CLASC to CLAT in 1971 was in keeping with the secular trend of the former Christian world labor movement.

So in the more flexible attitude toward the Communists and in its leftist tone the CLAT can be said to follow the line of its outside backers. Similarly the ORIT in its rigid anti-communism and in its comparatively more cautious ideological tone has expressed a position favored by its powerful outsiders the long-time enemies of communism in the AFL-CIO elite.

This being the case the ORIT-CLAT struggle can be viewed as one in which the main protagonists outside Latin America have set loose conflicting forces in the area of little positive consequence to the workers. From this perspective the struggle in Latin America is best seen as a bitter organizational fight fueled by outsiders and of doubtful value to the ordinary worker. The dependency of the weak *latino* affiliates upon their foreign backers for financial and other assistance, who lacking such aid would be drastically handicapped in their activities, reinforces the reasons for viewing the matter in this light.

There is however another way of looking at the picture that contributes to a fuller appreciation. Without denying the value in the view just explained this different perspective exposes important additional meanings. It suggests that this conflict does have a positive meaning for the ordinary workers—indeed for all Latin Americans. This significance exists, despite the comparatively limited popular effects of the labor bodies which each of the rivals heads. It exists despite the dependency of the ORIT and the CLAT for assistance upon outsiders.

The fundamental importance of the controversy is that it constitutes one more chapter in the continuing debate concerning how, given the political system of Latin America, changes vital to the workers' welfare are to be accomplished. Jáuregui and Máspero have expressed their particular version of the on-going question: reform or revolution? The ORIT leader is soberly optimistic as regards the achievement of far-reaching changes made within the rules of the political system. The CLAT leader reveals no such optimism.

Very few states in Latin America have the characteristics of legitimate nation-states. In other words very few are states whose peoples have for a long period of time displayed a commonness of unity founded upon a common history and a belief in a common destiny. In most states, also, the impersonal rule of law is lacking—whatever the formal constitutional and legislative enactments. Although some progress in this direction is evident, the figure of the leader, the *caudillio* (the dominant personality), is often the deciding factor. Politics is in the hands of the representatives of traditional interest groups to a degree not found in most western countries. The strength of these old groups comes from many sources in the rigidly stratified societies that are given to emulating the cultural model of the traditional elite classes.

It is against the background of this political system that Jáuregui and Máspero seek to make change. With this background in mind their claims must be weighed and judged. In their different fashions they are assigning to the workers a role in the aspirations for, and the means of, making the change. Furthermore, in their relations with their outside supporters they seek to use that support for Latin American ends. Their explanations of the relationship, the degree of success or failure in this enterprise, must also be judged.

The Conflicting Positions Summarized

The condition of Latin America being what it is each rival leader's approach may be deservedly praised—and criticized. There is evidence to suggest that although Latin American society is comparatively rigid, its political system has permitted the emergence of new contenders for power who are permitted to share in governmental decision-making. Labor is the prime example of new contender, which under the system has gained power and thus shared in the resources of the society, something previously denied to it. Accommodating to the political system labor has thus been admitted to the circle of accepted power contenders. In this manner it can be expected to continue to successfully push forward to further gains.

Contrariwise, there is also evidence that indicates the older interest groups by one means or other will not permit the new contender to really advance to a position of achieving its "legitimate" share of the society's resources. At best, say the critics, the traditional orders will partially yield before the new contender, but these concessions are insufficient to meet the ends—the welfare of the masses of the people. One cannot expect these ends to be achieved within the rules of the political system.

If this is saying that serious claims both for the viability of the system to transform itself, and also for the necessity of by-passing or violating the political system can be made, that is indeed the case. The Latin American situation is of that particular kind. In judging the conflicting positions of Jáuregui and Máspero the processes will be seen in this light. There will be much adding and subtracting, much averaging back and forth due to the inherent nature of the Latin American dilemma.

Judging Jáuergui

In Jáuregui's favor it would appear that from the way the Latin American political system operates, from what appears to be the views of the trade union leaders, and from a consideration of the normal political tactics of labor in seeking to improve its position, his pragmatic stance is worthwhile. The Latin American political system is one that admits new contenders into the political arena on the basis of displayed strength and on the basis of the understanding that the newcomers will not imperil the right of the traditional interests to share in the opportunity to exercise power. (And, it must be added, the new contenders must not threaten the destruction of what the older corporate groups regard as their essential interests.) Moreover, Latin American trade union leaders have become increasingly interested in basically economic concerns and less in political-ideological ones. Finally, the gains of labor have largely been made by pressure politics, by political bargaining with governments or parties. Jáuregui expounds a position that emphasizes dealing with the realities. He is in an organization of the most important and experienced trade unions in Latin America. These *latino* associates in the ORIT have for years followed the political banner of the populist so-called national revolutionary parties. Where these parties have been successful in electing representatives or governments, or as in the case of the Mexican PRI are the party which is identified with the government, labor has benefited. Participation in party politics has brought labor's representatives to the seats of power. It has put important trade union leaders among the highest ranks of the political elite. Using political pressure more often than collective bargaining (while also developing its sophistication in collective bargaining), the ORIT unions can be said to have successfully worked to the improvement of the workers welfare within the political system.

Jáuregui has been a part of this force. Persistently and stubbornly he has sought to move labor forward. For him labor is a power contender of stature—it has made its way into the seats of power, and while still not as powerful as the traditional interest groups, it is on the way up. It has seen the employers yield to its demands in the economic matters that are vital to its interests. And helping in the achievement of these gains, and in the building of democratic trade unionism have been the United States trade unions. Obviously much remains to be done, but what has been accomplished encourages a belief that with courage, determination, and hard work the workers can go on to greater achievements. The pragmatic view, with determined and persistent actions as the consequence of that pragmatism, represents an intelligent long view. Meaningful change, a gradual revolution, is possible. The workers are not likely to follow "extremists speaking from balconies" and risk losing their gains made within the system.

These are some of the arguments which favor the Jáuregui pragmatic "revolution through continuing fight for reforms." Certain things, however, need to be pointed out which dampen the acceptance of this approach. In essence the criticism argues that the populist road (which is really the one Jáuregui is taking) has been shown to be less promising than it originally seemed. In its years populism appeared to be the hope of the workers and admittedly gains have been made under the banner of the populist parties. But populism and the parties were, and are, essentially middle-class movements and in the end populism was willing to make its peace with the oligarchy at the expense of the ordinary workers. A politics of revolution-through-reforms has really come to serve the interest of a middle-class alliance with the oligarchy, while giving minimal and insufficient gains to the masses of workers, particularly the peasantry. This is the situation, for example, in Mexico ruled by the PRI, the party which also controls the Mexican labor movement and numbers the top leaders of Mexico (who are members of ORIT) in its hierarchy. The compromises of the populist *Apristas* in Peru, long supported by the big unions, has led to the formation of *Aprista rebelde* in reaction against the compromises. *Accion Democratica*, the populist party of Venezuela, has also been losing ground among the workers because of dissatisfaction with its achievements. In each of these instances the problem of whether satisfactory reforms in the interest of the masses of workers (*not* of the *elite* unions) can be achieved through the political system has been intensified.

In the Jáuregui-ORIT posture there seems too much concern for assuring orderly processes and working within the institutions when the needs of the masses of workers call for support of more radical party action committed to more sweeping programs than the ORIT has yet undertaken. But how, it might be asked, can this necessary shift be expected to come from a labor leader responsible to a regional organization composed of the kind of unions which make up the strength of ORIT? Are not these the most important unions in Latin America precisely because they are led by men who over the years have given up any former militancy and learned to deal and compromise with the oligarchy and the employers? In other words, for the most part ORIT is made up of unions and union leaders who have joined the system and were admitted to the ruling circles. How, under such circumstances, could Jáuregui reasonably be expected to advocate an extreme politics?

The ORIT leader, then, is following a politics that makes labor a pressure group with the good intentions of making labor a progressively strong intermediary at the centers of power. Whether or not the goal of satisfying the welfare of the ordinary workers can be achieved in this manner is questionable. No certain answer can be made for Latin American governments and political parties have always sought to co-opt labor for the government's use.

The relation of ORIT to the United States unions appears as more of a liability than an asset for a labor leader seeking identification in any meaningful way with changing the Latin American status quo. American trade unions are conservative organizations and for the most part cooperate with the United States government's policies in Latin America. (Indeed it is likely that the conservative American trade union leaders are the important contributors to U.S. policy concerning labor in Latin America.) A special study prepared for the U.S. Senate Committee on Foreign Relations, already referred to here, indicates that neither the American trade union complex of the U.S. Department of State relations vis à vis ORIT bring it much popular favor in Latin America.[1]

Yet despite these criticisms of the Jáuregui-led ORIT's pragmatic stance there is still something to be said in its favor. We will return to that after considering the Máspero-CLAT dealings with the Latin American political system.

Judging Máspero

Emilio Máspero is an avowed militant revolutionist. He has always emphasized the necessity of the organization he leads taking the combative political road. His early fight for the control of the CLASC revealed the differences between him and the previous moderate leadership. That leadership was anti-capitalist Christian, but it was concerned with more immediate trade unionism, and with strengthening relations with its few moderate and highly independent affiliates from the countryside. Máspero's political emphasis and militant message aimed at the many people among the workers in the country and the cities who were open to a radical non-Marxist appeal. These are people who are deeply dissatisfied with the present conditions and insistent on changes that constitute a social revolution. They, in contrast to the groups affiliated with the ORIT, include the newer and the weaker trade union groupings as well as nonunion workers. For the most part such people are extremely doubtful that the political system as it normally operates will permit the realization of their needs.

Máspero's avowed goal is social revolution and he has advocated a politics that has steadily moved in the direction of challenging the present system. Disavowing the so-called national revolutionary parties (the populists) for having really compromised with the traditional ruling classes, for some years he had CLASC functioning as a kind of unofficial auxiliary of the Christian Democratic parties in Chile and Venezuela. His rather brash claims concerning the importance of CLASC in contributing to the Christian Democrats presidential victory in Chile in 1964 were resented by the more moderate members of the party. Máspero's radical Christian humanism (which at times also had him in difficulties with churchmen who supported the Christian Democrats) was always in sympathy with the leftist elements of Christian Democracy.

Máspero was for years among the militant labor leaders of the Christian world movement who were pushing along the more militant road. Today, following the international line begun years ago in relinquishing a commitment as a labor organization to Christian religious principles, the CLAT provides its leader with a still greater opportunity to move further to the left. Today, as has been indicated, the Máspero-led CLAT disavows populism with even greater zeal than had CLASC. While it is friendly to the Christian Democratic parties of Chile and Venezuela (countries where Christian Democracy is strong), it has moved in a direction that no longer can be described simply as a kind of unofficial auxiliary of Christian humanism in politics. Sympathetic to radical Christian humanism and to Christian Democratic politics as it is, it is now a more radical independent organization in its tone and actions. Any means that is deemed helpful in advancing the cause of the workers as CLAT envisions it seems justified. This includes collaboration with Communists and other varieties of Marxists (with whom, as has been indicated, Máspero has keen philosophical differences), when such actions appear strategically beneficial. Politically, then, Máspero's road is one based upon radical eclecticism. He appeals to all (including members of ORIT over the heads of their leaders) who will aid him in organizing a new workers' movement, radically restructuring Latin American society. Highly critical of the way in which the great bulk of labor unions have accommodated to the system and as a result have brought only limited changes, Máspero disavows pragmatism and conducts a wide-sweeping attack against the social and political system. All else, including the admittedly important task of organizing trade unions, appears incidental to this major purpose.

This aggressive political, thrust which really questions the validity of the Latin American political system as one permitting meaningful change is, in light of the record, praiseworthy. The normal course of Latin American politics works within a milieu that is too restrictive to permit the necessary changes demanded by the depressed conditions of the masses. The institutions and understandings through which Latin American politics operates are those which, at bottom, favor the traditional groups, the oligarchy. The rules of the political game permit only modifications, not the substantial changes in the environment necessary for securing the ordinary worker's welfare. These modifications have been accepted by the majority of the Latin American trade union leaders who, rather than seeking to really change the environment, have elected to come to terms with it.

It should not be expected that under the prevailing circumstances much else than limited changes could be achieved. The point is that the circumstances will have to be altered—the rules of the game redrawn more in favor of the poorer classes. This is most difficult, if not impossible, to do by working within the boundaries set by normal politics. The example of present-day Chile, one of the few countries in Latin America with a democratic politics and a country in which the organized working class is politically significant, is a case in point. Sparked originally by Eduardo Frei and the Christian Democrats, and carried forward by the *Unidad Popular* of Marxist president Salvador Allende, a definite change is in progress. But the difficulties of carrying it forward are enormous and it is yet to be shown once and for all that they can be accomplished under the normal politics. Even if they were, through a majority of the people accepting drastic changes successfully carried out in the present constitutional processes, this would be untypical for Latin America as a whole. On the contrary it is extremely doubtful that throughout Latin America the political system would permit such changes.

In relation to the question of change within the present political system Máspero's criticisms of populism are for the most part well taken. And this despite his exaggerated charges that populism is the tool of an imperialist capitalism for manipulating the workers and frustrating popular revolutions. He claims that the machinations of capitalism halted the early revolutionary fervor of the populist leaders. That is far too simple an explanation for the eventual outcome of what were not worker, but middle-class, indigenous social movements. Nevertheless Máspero's criticisms of populist party politics are basically sound for reasons already indicated. Changes were made by the populist national revolutionary parties throughout Latin America, but they were for the most part those which the more flexible sector of the oligarchy was willing to accept. These changes represent a modus vivendi between the middle class and the accommodating oligarchy. In country after country where they worked within the normal politics, for one reason or other, these originally ardent parties of social revolution have faltered in the task of fundamentally restructuring their societies. And in Mexico, which eventually produced the PRI, the official party of a revolution made by violence, a new oligarchy of the middle class appears to have arisen which numbers among its adherents the elite labor leaders. Populism never could achieve the interests of the masses because it was a movement seeking change for the middle classes and not the masses.

Thus it would seem that a new militant challenge must be raised on the entire political front. A political party of the workers must come from the workers. Trade unions must return to their older, broadly political, intensely ideological ways and ardently press for meaningful change. The workers will not advocate violence but neither will they falter in their persistent agitation for a new social order. Experience shows that theirs is a class struggle in Latin America and that it must go on. In Latin America the class lines are drawn more sharply than in the more socially and politically advanced Western countries.

Under the conditions prevailing in Latin American politics, temporary alliances or agreements with all elements that in one fashion or other contribute to a militant politics which aids the workers may be defended as viable. In such conditions it is sensible to hold a dialogue with Marxists of different stripes, to applaud certain efforts of the present Marxist regime in Chile even if doctrinally one is opposed to Marxism. What counts, at least in the short run, is moving with those who oppose the present order.

Viewed in this light, Máspero's position is attractive. Yet when we turn again to weighing all the factors—the reactions that such a politics might provoke and the possible consequences which might follow a drastic change, there is reason enough to hesitate. Either in reactions to radical politics, or where a radical revolution presumably in the name of the people took place in recent Latin American history, the results have been a new form of authoritarian political order with the trade unions still controlled by the state. The various revolutionary military juntas (including the newer Latin American version of Nasserism) or Cuba's *Fidelismo*; none of these represent the democratic socialism communitarianism, the kind of change Máspero agitates for. The example afforded by these regimes indicate a need to proceed more cautiously and pragmatically within the political system. Jáuregui believes that in this way there is a much better chance of labor developing as a strong autonomous democratic group.

Ideology Again

Looking at Latin American realities no simple answer can be given in favor of the politics of Jáuregui or of Máspero. It is difficult to comprehend how the present political system can be made to serve the interests of the submerged masses, in most countries the majority of the population. A total reconstruction of the system seems necessary if the job is to be done, and an essentially democratic society achieved. Yet it is equally difficult to be sure that an extremist politics will not lead to a newer kind of domination of the masses. Moreover, it is very difficult to discover where in most countries there exists a definite will among the masses to assure the militant social revolutionary leader who is pledged to democracy the support which will reasonably give him the victory.

Whatever doubts arise in the light of this grim scene concerning the respective manners in which Máspero and Jáuregui see the political system, the constant attention which Máspero has given to the importance of ideology weighs in his favor. The Latin American conditions, with its misery for the many, its rewards for the few—in other words its division into more polarized sectors—is one demanding that a social movement seeking to arouse the enthusiasm and support of the masses be an ideologically-oriented one. The labor movement should be a force that helps concretize the inarticulate desires of the people for change and which guides that change along democratic lines. The labor movement must explain to its followers and to the masses what constitutes reality, how it may be changed, and what will follow. As a militant radical democratic movement, labor must underscore the democratic basis of its organization and indicate that it intends to replace the oligarchy with democracy.

As we have seen Máspero has always been an ideological person. His fervent belief in ideology expressed from the beginning of his entrance into CLASC continued throughout the years and goes on during the present reincarnation of the formerly Christian movement into CLAT. In CLAT he is carrying forward, with what might be called a more secular emphasis, the radical Christian humanism which was the foundation of the CLASC ideology.

Whatever caveats may be entered in examining Máspero's ideological message the overall verdict must be a favorable one. Without subscribing to all of its content one must be impressed with its attention to the causes of what so many specialists call the contemporary social revolution that is either in process or struggling to be born throughout Latin America. And from the functional standpoint—in offering a common mirror to the workers in which they see themselves, comprehend their society, and are infused with a sense of mission—Máspero's belief system deserves high marks indeed.

The message presents the cause of social revolution in the reality of the Latin American condition. The existing social, political, legal, and economic institutions are exposed as those favoring the old or new oligarchies. Latin America is seen as an area in which the basic needs of the masses, the fundamental material requirements for a dignified life, are denied. This is the reason for the social revolution which is manifest in different degrees throughout the area.

In his explanation Máspero hits hard at the native oligarchies, but he is equally, perhaps even more virulent in holding certain outside nations responsible for the situation. The native oligarchies and their henchmen are the collaborators of foreign rich countries—particularly the United States—who act to maintain the internal as well as external conditions of colonialism. The Latin American workers learn from bitter everyday experience the consequences of this colonialism. Their experiences move them to struggle, to continue to organize and move relentlessly toward consummating a genuine social revolution. This eventual victory can be, will be, achieved. The depressed masses are capable of being aroused and will support a workers' movement that is infused with a high morality. Having this moral orientation CLAT (CLASC) is a workers' body that identified itself with the interests of the masses and does not betray them by accepting minimal changes and a position within the system.

In his analysis of the cause for the Latin American social revolution and explanations of the workers primary role in bringing it to fruition Máspero stresses the need for true democracy within the workers organization. He asserts that the wellsprings of the organized force that spearhead the drive for fundamental change, lie within the ordinary workers themselves. Only a movement which, at bottom, comes from the workers and is responsible to them is justified. In its ideological statements Máspero's position is one of great optimism concerning the workers contributions to the social revolutionary program.[2] It is thus a strongly democratic message. Moreover, as has been shown, it is an ideology which emphasizes moral superiority over any materialist position. Man's desire to better his condition, to grow to a dignified human being, is the prevailing note. This moral end is not just a rationalization for seeking material gain, although assuredly material gains are essential to the securing of the moral end.

Máspero's ideological effort also meets the test of being functionally sound. It is a belief system that suggests to the workers an explanation of the reasons for their depressed conditions. It is optimistic in its view that the eventual victory—the replacement of the oligarchic society by a democratic society—can take place. It has its villains and its heroes. It warns of the obstacles along the road to success. It says that the road will not be easy. Those taking it will be menaced by powerful enemies at home and abroad. Great sacrifices will be demanded. But in the end the workers will prevail and the new society will be attained. Infused with the rightness of their cause, bolstered by high moral support from a militant non-religious "Christian" humanism, the workers have aligned themselves with the winning side in their battle with the Powers of Darkness. It must not be forgotten that this is a message coupled with a distinct appeal to *latino* pride and *dignidad*. Only the workers can save the workers, and to this task only Latin Americans are called. Only Latin Americans can truly understand the Latin American predicament. No matter what other sources of aid are available, in the end only Latin Americans can and must do the job.

In stressing the importance of ideology and in his contributions to the belief system of the CLAT (CLASC) Máspero, and his adherents, have performed a distinct service. Latin American labor, if it has wanted to speak for the masses, has in recent decades lacked a fighting dynamic message aimed at stirring the impulses of the millions of ordinary men and women. The inclination of the workers to aspire toward change and a democratic society makes Máspero's call attractive.

Jáuregui strives to strengthen trade unionism as a special interest group which becomes powerful enough to enter the circle of decision-making in the system and thus act in the workers interests; Máspero denies that such a way is helpful. He says that it is futile, if the interests of the *masses* of workers are what labor leaders are truly seeking to advance. Of course Máspero, heading a smaller, more heterogeneous, radical group, can afford an absolute commitment to change of the most profound kind. Jáuregui, by the very nature of his organization, has a more difficult job to do in constructing an ORIT ideology.

The special conference in January 1971, which spent a good deal of time discussing ideology, illustrates some of the problems Jáuregui faces. At that conference several voices were raised sounding a more militant note—criticizing capitalism, the great powers, and praising socialism. But while these more radical expressions were indicative of a great inclination to openly express long-held impulses they were the expressions of a minority in a very autonomous labor international. To further truly understand the picture it must be remembered that the speakers who took the more radical position were all vehement critics of what they saw as the Social Christianity and clericalism of CLASC.

It must be said, therefore, that Jáuregui cannot be blamed for the ORIT's lack of a unifying clarion call expressing its ideological position. To repeat, he is secretary general of a politically prudent organization whose few more militant voices are, like the moderates, bitterly hostile to CLAT. Finally it is an organization whose big affiliates are well aware of its autonomous nature and express themselves freely—and often not in chorus.

It is now appropriate to make certain explanations in order to avoid possible misinterpretations of the analysis of Máspero's ideology which has just been presented. This is to say that caveats must be entered—questioning parts of the total belief system. We refer, for example, to his oversimplified explanations of United States policy and that of the AFL-CIO and the ORIT as agents of an exploitative capitalism, his vision of a new, single, Latin American state, and his demand that socialism is the kind of social order that the present social revolution must produce.

One can certainly agree with Máspero's charges that capitalism in Latin America has been highly exploitative both of natural and human resources and that it has in the main operated to concentrate wealth and power in the hands of the few to the detriment of the many. Again one can agree that theAFL-CIO, AIFLD, and to a lesser degree Latin Americans in the high councils of the ORIT, have asserted a strongly favorable attitude toward capitalism. Furthermore, the United States government's policy, being that of the largest capitalist country in the world, is assuredly friendly to the interests of American business in Latin America. (And often to an extent which in its lack of sensitivity to *latino* feelings is most justifiably open to criticism.) To say all this, however, is not to say what the Máspero-CLAT (CLASC) message says, namely, that the U.S. government, the U.S. labor elite, and the ORIT are in some kind of league to deliberately perpetuate the exploitative characteristics of capitalism. One might reject the belief of those in labor and government that free enterprise is *essential* to free labor (as this writer does) and still comprehend why the adherents of capitalism, themselves, think as they do. The AFL-CIO, for example, is the product of a history of American labor's fight against the exploitative features of capitalism. Máspero in certain of his statements shows that he is aware of this. But when he attacks his labor opponents for their activities in Latin America, along with his attacks on United States policy, he makes them all more or less conscious allies in fostering an exploitative economy throughout the area.

When this oversimplification of the actions of his opponents is joined with a real and virulent anti-*yanquism* (despite qualifications), the positive suggestiveness of the truth of the ideology is cheapened. It becomes demagoguery. The reader may, of course, feel that in his ideology Máspero is not presenting a professor's critique before some academic body but addressing another and far more important audience. He is, it can be argued, seeking to move a people whose nationalism is closely linked with an anti-capitalist, anti-imperialist outlook, an audience favorably disposed by history to the belief that United States government and native collaborators with the *yanquis* are responsible for Latin America's ills. Despite this, and despite the important truths contained in this point of view, it is not hair-splitting to assert that the Máspero-CLAT view is in some respects oversimplified and even erroneous.

Nationalism, Nation-hood

The CLAT (CLASC) ideology also puts forth a mystique that has its origins in the days of the early revolutions against Spain—the dream of a single huge Latin American nation. There are positive aspects in this appeal. It is attractive to the popular nationalism which in recent decades has come to spread throughout the area replacing the older aristocratic nationalism. Moreover, in support of this goal is the fact that there is a greater fundamental unity existing in Latin America than in any continent in the world. The Iberian heritage, with its closely related languages, common religion, and the characteristic social structure, has resulted in a uniformity not found elsewhere in such a huge land mass. Economic factors also exert an increasing pressure for common planning and integration.

At the same time the elements of diversity are such as to make unrealistic for a very long time, if ever, the realization of a single Latin American nation. Differences in history, size, geography, ethnic origins, and race abound. Indians, Spanish, Portuguese, and blacks are the basic ingredients producing the people. These basic strains have intermixed in various degrees. Mingling and/or mixing with the earlier stocks have come immigrants from Europe and Asia. Latin America is indeed an exotic mixture of peoples. In most countries the majority population is *mestizo*, Indian-white mixture, but there are also so many various intermixing combinations of race and nationality differences that it is erroneous to think of Latin Americans per se, as *mestizos*. And in a few countries there is little of the radical intermixtures that is characteristic of the region as a whole. Argentina and Uruguay, for example, are more "white" than is the United States.

These racial differences are important factors of diversity inasfar as the building of the national societies of the nations presently existing. They would intensify in all probability as problems in the case of making a nation out of the continent. Whatever the progress in racial tolerance that has been made, no matter how in some instances (in Mexico and Peru for example) the Indian has been extolled, the non-Indian (and the black) are inferiors. The *Aprista* call for one large nation which was accompanied by the glorification of the indigenous peoples, while arousing great enthusiasm throughout the continent, did so in many countries mainly as a symbol of independence from foreigners and as a challenge to Latin Americans to modernize their societies.

National differences are also reflected political creeds. Fidel Castro's communism, for example, for all of its characteristics making it a variant of communism particularly in the *latino* rather than the more Leninist pattern, soon ran into difficulties with Communists in other countries. These concerned doctrinal interpretations, strategies, and tactics, particularly where the *Fidelistas* sought to use their Cuban experiences as the guidelines that Communist leaders in other countries must follow.

In brief, the achievement of nationality and of nation-statehood by individual countries in Latin America has itself been a difficult matter. The unity that develops in a people resulting from a belief that they are joined in a common destiny which is expressed by a state to which all owe loyalty has had slow going in Latin America. Several countries, Costa Rica, Chile, Argentina, Uruguay, perhaps Mexico, have achieved such unity. Paraguay, the Dominican Republic, Nicaragua, Honduras, and El Salvador exhibit the most sluggish development of integrative features. The other countries lie somewhere in between. And within all the nations there exists in greater or lesser degree the profound differences between the educated, articulate, comparatively few living in modern society and the vast, inarticulate, deprived *pueblo* of the primitive society. Two "nations" or more exist within the same territorial boundaries of each country.

The different Latin American countries, then, appear to have enough to do for the indefinite long future to build truly national societies within their own borders. Máspero's appeal does have a positive aspect where it stimulates continental pride and independence in relation to the outside world. (The practical manifestations of this sense of *dignidad* are the increasingly unwillingness of Latin American nations to allow the United States to take them for granted in hemispheric and world affairs, and the movements for regional economic planning and integration.) In the light of all the evidence, however, Máspero's demand for a single continental state is farfetched. It will remain a topic around which copious oratory will continue to flow in the future as it has in the past.

Economics and Socialist Communitarianism

We move now to examine critically the economic basis of the new social order envisioned by the CLAT leader. This is to be socialism. What is called socialist communitarianism is a democratic form of socialism. Máspero, it will be recalled, is most emphatic in excluding capitalism in any shape or form as an economic order that the workers can accept. New and different adaptations of capitalism, i.e., neo-capitalism, are subject to bitter criticisms. The workers are warned that neo-capitalism is the guise in which the old order endeavors to bamboozle them, to hoodwink them into thinking that improvements are really being accomplished. They are told by Máspero that neo-capitalism is a tool by which capitalism seeks to frustrate the people's revolution, which carries with it the promise of democratic socialism. Let the workers, he says, beware the appearance of neo-capitalism!

Here again is a situation in which I, while accepting Máspero's basic criticisms of native and foreign business practices in Latin America, and sympathizing with his rejection of capitalism in favor of socialism, cannot by any means agree entirely with him. To be sure one can understand why Máspero should feel as he does about capitalism and thus warn the workers against neo-capitalism. A look at the history of capitalist practices, native and foreign, in Latin America is all that is needed for that comprehension. One can also favor socialism over capitalism as a socioeconomic order. But to say this is not at all inconsistent with severely questioning Máspero's views. For it does not follow that because of the way capitalism has basically operated in the past in Latin America that neo-capitalism is bound to continue in the same course. It does not follow that socialism is the necessary and only successor to the old bad capitalism—that socialism alone is the wave of the new future order.

It is indeed a reasonable assumption that what Latin America needs as a result of social revolution is a democratic neo-capitalism. This neo-capitalism rather than being the bridge to serve the old capitalism might even be the bridge to an eventual socialism. Or it might be a "mixed economy" of individual enterprise cooperatives, public planning, and socialism in various degrees.

In view of the prevailing systems in most Latin American countries, as well as the scope of the changes that would be involved, any insistence that the new order must be socialist, that neo-capitalism is per se unacceptable, is unrealistic—and even dangerous. This is so not only because such intransigence could in a crisis provoke a successful reaction from the oligarchy supported by its domestic and foreign friends. Even if the adherents of socialism came to power there is the likelihood that a new form of suppression might well be the result. Latin

American realities, unfortunately, make this doleful prediction a distinct possibility. The history of a devotion to, and practice of, the rule of impersonal law is not a very impressive one. Nor is the record of democracy as being the way in which, above all others, the exercise of power is legitimized. The insistence on only socialism, the moving of the people toward socialism, might entail highly authoritarian procedures which, particularly in such societies, would be the very least endanger the nourishing of the democratic way.

Under such conditions what would probably happen would be that an authoritarian socialism would be brought into thy new order but the order would be proclaimed as a democratic one. So the world would witness still another revolution in which an exploitative capitalism, piously held by its adherents to be the root of a democratic society, was replaced by an authoritarian socialism whose devotees insisted with even greater fervor that now democracy had triumphed! [3]

Victor Alba has considered this problem of the need to replace the old capitalism with a different economic system. It lies at the heart of the necessity of replacing an oligarchic society with a democratic one. Alba affirms that classical capitalism has failed but, he says, that in view of circumstances prevailing in Latin America this doesn't mean that what will replace classical capitalism will necessarily turn out to be an economic order which will nuture democracy.

Alba himself affirms the need in Latin America for a dynamic ideology which presses for a different type of capitalism from the classical capitalism. It is a capitalism which exists alongside government ownership of the essential sources of wealth, a capitalism permitting and encouraging private profit in a society where the government legislates to insure a fundamentally equitable distribution of goods and income. Political democracy must also be nurtured.

This democratic, neo-capitalist social order, Alba says, is what Latin America should aim at. It would constitute the major part of a truly revolutionary ideology. To be sure there is always the possibility that the oligarchical and other anti-democratic supporters of classical capitalism will not accept the proposed change. The dangers involved in seeking this radical change are great—and not only from the old orders, but from the various authoritarian ones which seek to replace them. But, he says, the risk is always great in any radical proposal.[4]

The point of Alba's type of proposal is that what he is suggesting is more in keeping with Latin American needs and the realities of Latin American politics—meaning the possibilities of making some kind of meaningful change within the society without losing all hope for democracy—than is Máspero's way. Alba's type of proposal, a revision of capitalism with limitations on the power of the present ruling sector that it would entail, would bring about a fundamental social reconstruction. It would set in motion a genuine revolution while involving less risk to freedom than the sweeping socialist alternative demanded by Máspero. In addition it could possibly become a progressive transition en route to an eventual socialism in the indefinite future.

It is here again that Jáuregui's more eclectic views are suggestive of what in most Latin American countries may constitute the future. Over the years while paying compliments to what really constituted a modified capitalism he also indicated that the *different* economic beliefs represented in the ORIT must not be forgotten. More and more today he stresses an eclectic position, admitting the value in a democratic socialism, where previously he dwelt more upon the importance of a modified capitalism. His more moderate approach underscores the value of a "mixed economy" of a new form of "capitalism," increasing governmental controls in the public interest and "socialism." Jáuregui, like Máspero, knows that Latin America for the most part is still at the introductory stage of capitalism. Unlike his rival he believes that it is at the present time better for Latin America not to disdain and attack capitalism but to reconstitute it in ways that will serve the people. To be sure Jáuregui's way may be overly optimistic as regards the willingness of the capitalists to change. But any move toward important change involves risk. And Jáuregui's willingness to accept a type of neo-capitalism seems more likely in most of the countries to possibly sustain the slender thread of democracy than does Máspero's adamant demands for the complete obliteration of capitalism.

Again Those "Outsiders"

The fact that each of our rival labor leaders and their respective organizations have powerful foreign supporters also is a major—some would say *the* major—element in the story of this conflict. In multiple ways this outside relationship has affected the life of ORIT and of CLASC. It will continue to be so in the future.

We have seen how the charges and countercharges over the years have made it appear that each leader and his organization are the pliable agents or agencies of their particular foreign backers. (This charge is most frequently made in one form or other as regards Jáuregui and ORIT.) Each is said to so depend upon the bounty of the outsiders that each acts in accordance with the wishes if not outright directions of people located in Europe and the United States.

These mutual recriminations from the protagonists of each conflicting organization can be expected to continue indefinitely into the future. Conversations in December 1972, in Mexico City and Cuernavaca, Mexico, at ORIT hemispheric headquarters and that of FAT (*Frente Autentico del Trabajo*), the Mexican affiliate of CLAT, bear out this prediction.[5] The way in which the whole matter affects the views of interested nonpartisans, and the important multiple effects that the relationship makes upon the leaders and their organizations, entitles the matter to careful perusal.

The degree of financial support from the outside is difficult to ascertain. Various backers, actually or supposedly, underwriting the rival organizations have already been cited in this study. Obviously it is agreed by innumerable qualified observers that foreign financial backing of significance has been, and is, an important source of the means by which ORIT and CLAT can operate.

Be all this as it may the position taken here in judging the effects of the outside relationship is from the outset to reject any view that directly or indirectly says that the circumstances of Latin American labor weakness and wealthy backers from abroad makes either Jáuregui or Máspero the servant of foreign masters. Their agreements with their foreign benefactors spring from other causes. The degree to which their bills may be paid does not make them the agents of outsiders any more than the presumed or actual Cuban dependency upon Russia makes Fidel Castro the leader of a Soviet puppet satellite.

Indeed it is difficult to conceive of either Jáuregui or Máspero being in any fashion the tools of others. Jáuregui, fundamentally in accord with the AFL-CIO, AIFLD, and the world organization ICFTU, a *latino* definitely inclined to cooperation with the United States, has been quick to assert the autonomy of ORIT and to insist upon the primacy of ORIT interests over all other considerations. Forced by circumstances to move carefully in dealing with the powerful U.S. labor elements in ORIT he has consistently endeavored to make clear that the Latin American trade unions within ORIT existed like the AFL-CIO before ORIT, that they on their own initiative helped to form or entered ORIT because they felt they had common objectives with the United States unions. Admittedly the AFL-CIO is richer and more powerful than the Latin members. Jáuregui, however, has always insisted that such bodies as the Mexican CTM, the Venezuelan CTV, the CTP of Peru—examples of some of the most important Latin American unions in ORIT—are not controlled by the AFL-CIO.

As has been indicated the overriding American concern of the North American trade unions with combating communism in Latin America was in some degree shared by the Latin American trade unions. This, and not the AFL-CIO wishes in the matter, has been the reason for ORIT policy. Jáuregui and the other *latino* leaders may be wrong in having put such an emphasis upon combating communism. (I have always believed *ORIT*'s emphasis in this matter has been misplaced.) But this view was essentially their view as well as that of the powerful big brothers of the AFL-CIO. Moreover, in their relationship one feels that Jáuregui and other *latinos*, although believing in the anti-Communist line, were more concerned with using ORIT as an instrumentality of building trade unionism throughout Latin America and fostering the growth of fledging democracy within that trade union development.

Again, as has been indicated in this book, Jáuregui, the good friend of the American labor elite, has not hesitated to criticize his friends when he disagreed with them and to assert the *latino* position. Anyone who watched Jáuregui work over the years for the establishment of the labor college at Cuernavaca—and for a time against the tide of the powers that be within the AFL-CIO and AIFLD, knows this.[6] His administration has been one that insists on the primacy of loyalty to ORIT from all its officials. Where he felt that such was not being demonstrated by Americans attached to ORIT headquarters he went so far as to discharge at least one such official. "We Latin Americans in ORIT are very good friends of the Americans. That is why we can be at times their critics." "I respect George Meany and Jay Lovestone, but Washington is not Rome and neither of my friends are the pope." "We Latin Americans are friends of our American friends, but we are no colonials." These and similar expressions Jáuregui has repeated to this author over the many years he has been secretary general of ORIT.

Friend of U.S. labor, but demanding mutual respect, he has also taken the same attitude with regards to the U.S. government. He is as we have seen a Latin American who believes that it is essential to seek cooperation with the United States. Given the deep cultural differences between the peoples of Latin America and the United States, and the difference in power between *el coloso* and the Latin American countries, the task is enormous. For Jáuregui, however, the hard pragmatic facts tell him that the effort to achieve understanding and cooperation must continually be made. So he works at the job while at the same time he endeavors to present the Latin American view. On occasion his assertions of a Latin American sense of independence can be bluntly made. Such an occasion is illustrated in his comments following the United States presidential elections of November 1972. The Mexico City newspaper *El Universal* for November 9, under the heading "No Intresó a Sectores Obreros," quoted the secretary general of ORIT as follows:

The Republicans and the Democrats of the United States see the problems of Latin America as something far away in which they take no interest. It makes no difference to us who is elected. The only thing that we are able to hope for is not that Nixon will help us, but that he will not obstruct the development programs of the Latin American countries.[7]

The principle focus of those who regard ORIT and Jáuregui as too dominated by influences outside Latin America has overwhelmingly been centered upon the connections with the United States government and the AFL-CIO and AIFLD. Regarding the contacts between the global labor body to which ORIT affiliates, the ICFTU, which is located in Brussels, little has been said by the critics. Yet during the regime of Luis Alberto Mongé, Jáuregui's predecessor in the office of secretary general, there was at times bitter dissension between the ICFTU and ORIT. The regional organization claimed that its autonomy was being interfered with from Brussels. Jáuregui following Mongé continued to assert the autonomy of the Latin American organization and eventually the differences were ended.

Jáuregui has drawn upon the ICFTU's common solidarity fund for financial assistance in support of constructing ORIT's labor college in Cuernavaca, and in conducting its programs. Along with other brother foreign union agencies he has used the services of ICFTU in bolstering ORIT programs. At times in talking with him one gained the impression that he was looking to ICFTU (along with national confederations such as the Canadian one) for various kinds of assistance to bolster some kind of independence from his friends in the affluent United States trade unions.[8]

Máspero, like Jáuregui, has always emphasized the autonomy of his Latin American organization in its relations with its helpful friends from abroad. As Jáuregui has called attention to the initiative of certain anti-Communist Latin American trade union confederations in joining with their AFL-CIO brethren in forming ORIT, so Máspero points to the initiative of Latin American Christian labor groupings and individuals in organizing CLASC. CLASC was born largely, he says, because of Latin Americans who were not interested in being part of the labor extension of the cold war represented most forcefully in the Western Hemisphere by the CTAL versus ORIT. CLASC had its origins in groupings of exclusively Latin American workers interested in being free from any alignments with imperialist power blocs, i.e., the super powers of the world. In Latin America, the CTAL and ORIT, which sought to dominate the labor scene according to Máspero, were definitely aligned with the big powers.

The former world Christian labor international, the IFCTU, not being associated with the super powers, but on the contrary having its strength among smaller European states, offered the natural international "parenthood" for the kind of Christian trade unionism that developed out of a Latin American initiative. The qualities of the much smaller IFCTU were those that the Latin American workers interested in freedom of ideas and action (autonomy) could appreciate. The former IFCTU also offered a means for the poor Latin American workers to make contacts with their equally poor and anti-imperialist brothers in the other parts of the Third World in Asia and Africa.

It was, says Máspero, in effect quite in keeping with the forces already at work within the then IFCTU that it should have changed its ethic from one of Christian humanism to one of a universal humanism. The new WCL represents to an even greater extent a Third World labor international free of compromises with imperialist powers and devoted to fostering the solidarity of the autonomous regional affiliates. CLAT, successor to CLASC in Latin America, rejoices in its membership in the WCL. Such a world labor body can (as the other two world labor groupings because of their alignments never can) construct and build solidarity between the workers of the Third World.[9]

Máspero has demonstrated his own initiative within the circles of the world movement with which he affiliates on several occasions. At world conferences and elsewhere he was one of the main figures in urging the former IFCTU to take a more militant and universalistic road. His audacity and independence were noted by both his supporters and his critics within the then world Christian labor movement. There was never anything of the supplicant or the moderate in the posture of the ebullient, charismatic Máspero. His stance was always one reflecting his belief that the relation between the Latin American groupings and the IFTCU was that of co-equals. The Europeans had resources, but so did he, although his were not to be measured in money. They were of a kind that could rouse the interests of the masses, of the poor and exploited in the making of a needed social revolution. He would rally those workers in Latin America who rejected the domination of the cold war labor antagonists—the Communists and ORIT.

It must be acknowledged that there have been very few of Máspero's European backers that have sought to brake his fervent policies and appeals. His outright critics, the few he had, have been overruled. Among his backers behind-the-scenes there are those who at times deplore his rashness, his reckless attacks. They may shake their heads wistfully over the descent into demagoguery. But they themselves believe in the militant course that he helped to construct for the former Christian world labor movement.

In the matter of having important outside supporters in a Latin America whose people in the last decades have become increasingly sensitive to any such influences, Máspero has less to explain than does Jáuregui. His European supporters come from smaller countries, or at least from countries that are not as negatively perceived as is the United States, the country which is seen as the main source of Jáuregui's outside support. Again, Máspero's foreign supporters are assisting a militant movement for social change. The foreign supporters of Jáuregui appear more cautious with regard to change. To some people in Latin America ORIT's outside supporters have failed to appreciate the native workers impulse for change and democracy and have been too concerned with opposing communism. Moreover, Máspero's various European backers befriend a purely native movement, not a mixed bag of *latinos* and affluent *yanquis*. In many sectors of the populace *yanquis* are by definition menacingly powerful, if not bad, neighbors. This view of the United States as the "big neighbor" (whether good or bad) who always seeks in different ways to control the hemisphere is omnipresent.

Jáuregui's relations, then, with his outside benefactors are more complicated. He has a more difficult task than does his rival in explaining and justifying his outside connections. In addition to the anti-*gringoism* arising from the unhappy history of the inter-American relations there has been for years the cold war with all of its ramifications including the long U.S. involvement in Vietnam. In this cold war and in the Vietnamese conflict the leaders of the AFL-CIO have been among the most prominent proponents for attacking communism wherever found, making no distinction between the various communisms extant in today's world. Moreover, in a Latin America where capitalism is at least more subject to question, the AFL-CIO's and AIFLD's comfortable identification with capitalism, their at times insensitivity to Latin American impulses, their honest convictions that American labor values and American labor techniques are the best for the *latinos*—all of these matters pose problems for Jáuregui, within the singular Latin American milieu, that his rival does not confront.

I have treated the problems arising within ORIT and the American labor supporters in some detail elsewhere.[10] Most of the difficulties mentioned eight years ago continue to exist. These include the conflicts that arise within ORIT because of its inter-American membership; the U.S. unionists overriding concern with communism; U.S. labor's defense of capitalism as essential to freedom in a part of the world where workers are more inclined to criticizing capitalism; the cooperation of U.S. labor and business in a milieu where there is difficulty in understanding such a relation; U.S. labor leadership's failure to fully understand the desire for destroying semi-feudal society.

In brief these differences result from the underlying values of people who are products of societies with different social structures and different political, scientific, and technological development. I would continue to argue that the most important single fact in Latin America today is social revolution—meaning the movement to destroy a semi-feudal society—that appears in one fashion or other. (U.S. union leaders have not been the only Americans from the United States operating in Latin America that have failed to understand this.)

It is ironic that *yanqui* unionists, believers in liberal capitalism, products of a tradition that fought the classical exploitative capitalism of their own country, should in their fears of communism obstruct a politics that might be part of a progressive capitalist democratic revolution.

The affluent, successful U.S. unionists, products of a different history, have labored long and diligently to help their *latino* brothers achieve goals that Americans from the United States believe in. Their practical experience in the United States has taught them these means and ends are best. The teaching of collective bargaining, trade union formal education in opposition to anti-democratic politics (which in *practice* has, at times, meant siding with conservative authoritarian orders and a suspicion of liberals and/or leftists of any persuasion who are not flatly opposing communists), the insistence that capitalism and freedom are inseparable, is accompanied by the use of money and technical assistance to aid those unions accepting the *yanqui* unionist's particular beliefs of what is good. All this is done among comparatively poor people. Much of what the representatives of U.S. labor strive for is in itself not bad. The question is, is it effectively working toward the end that Latin American workers—given their particular *ambiente*—should aspire to; that is, the destruction of a semi-feudal society; the overthrow of the oligarchy in favor of democracy. In its various policies beginning in 1954 and later in Guatemala, in the Dominican Republic, in Brazil, and in Cuba, the AFL-CIO in one fashion or other fought what to its leaders was the principal menace—the threat of Communist or Communist-supported political movements which would destroy trade union freedom. To many Latin American workers the menace was not so apparent, or at least not as much so as was the menace to freedom represented by those whom the Communists, along with far more non-Communists, opposed at the time.

The Future

With the recent indications that the fires of the cold war are being dampened the AFL-CIO leadership is presented with a new opportunity to turn away from its sterile major concern with fighting communism as the key to building democratic trade unionism. The Americans can give the lie to Máspero's charge that ORIT only serves their purposes as a cold war instrument. They should still continue their assistance to ORIT, but extensively revise their policies. Their support within ORIT should be of a kind that does not compromise Jáuregui's efforts to direct that organization's efforts into more productive channels in the difficult task of following the evolutionary route to accelerated change in Latin America.

It would help Jáuregui if the AFL-CIO would divest itself of those associations with American business corporations and the American government which—for whatever reasons—give it a bad image in Latin America. Specifically this would mean a drastic change within the American Institute for Free Labor Development. That agency should become less dependent upon business and governmental funding and seek sources of income less likely to be questioned in Latin America. Its budget and the extent of its activities would be reduced, but this does not mean that it would become a less effective force in helping to build a native democratic trade unionism. Both the amounts of money it spends and the sources of the AIFLD funds have been criticized by many people inside and outside Latin America who consider themselves friends of American labor. These friendly critics believe that the AIFLD spends far too much money, and spends it ineffectively. Too much reliance is put on money and the emoluments that the wealthy AIFLD can provide in the field and, particularly, in Washington D.C., and the AIFLD "graduate center" in Ft. Royal, Virginia. Such a condition, say these critics, can have an insidious effect upon people coming out of the humble circumstances of most workers in the Latin American labor movement.

A leaner budget, with most of it going to the kind of work AIFLD has been doing in its Social Projects Division, and the gradual transferring of most of its workers' education and more narrowly concerned trade union activity development work to ORIT, would bring more effective help to Jáuregui and his organization in the future. The use of the experienced AIFLD personnel in workers' education should continue, but under formal ORIT jurisdiction.

Such a reorganization of AIFLD, together with that of an ORIT more definitely oriented to Latin American interests, would remove many of the problems that bedevil Jáuregui before Latin America—and throughout the world.

It would destroy his critics' contention that ORIT is little more than a cold war instrument of the United States. It would end the unhappy current situation in which the far wealthier AIFLD is in effect the rival of ORIT, the regional organization with which the AFL-CIO affiliates. Centering the educational activities of training young Latin American workers, and of all who wished to contribute to that activity in Cuernavaca (and thus removing the competition from Washington, D.C.) would not only increase the prestige of Latin Americans but, hopefully, contribute to a more indigenously-shaped program.

Obviously all of this change would require that AFL-CIO people concerned with Latin America be willing to change their minds and also to sacrifice some of their power. There are at the present time within the AFL-CIO, according to Jáuregui, a minority which insists on using the power of the U.S. affiliate to try to put ORIT on a particular political course of which this minority approves. These people believe that if ORIT will not follow such politics—and Jáuregui says that he will not—then the regional organization should be abandoned. There are others, however, among the wealthy AFL-CIO who could be open to the friendly persuasion to make the changes suggested here. William Doherty, Jr., director of AIFLD, an experienced Latin Americanist, highly respected by Latin Americans with whom he relates closely, might be willing to move in this new direction even though it really means transferring AIFLD resources to ORIT and curtailing his own organization's activities.[11]

If something along the lines suggested here were to take place in the future the powerful U.S. labor movement would be truly supporting Jáuregui in the hard task of seeking meaningful change through working within the Latin American political system. Such action would most likely mean that change would move in the direction that Victor Alba, as we have seen, feels would be truly revolutionary in the area—that of creating a democratic capitalistic society. Surely such a change should find favor with the U.S. government, the U.S. public, as well as American business men of vision.

Under such conditions the conflict between Jáuregui and Máspero would continue, but in a fashion more productive to Latin American interests—and hopefully at a higher intellectual level. Jáuregui would be building towards democracy without insisting that it be linked to any one type of economic order although a neo-capitalist democracy would most likely evolve in most instances. Jáuregui would continue to steer clear of communism in his politics, but this would be incidental to his emphasis upon developing democracy, and no longer appear to be the major concern. His CLAT rival would seek a democracy also, but one pledged to socialism. While disagreeing with Communists and other Marxists he would not be opposed to common action with them where he believed that such action aided in progress toward the social revolution.[12] The change which might result from a major shift in AFL-CIO policies in Latin America should lessen the mutual recriminations that have too often character- ized the Jáuregui-Máspero conflict and given it the deceptive appearance of amounting to nothing more significant than a personal feud. Hopefully the conflict would become more of a dialogue concerning the means of change in Latin America and the workers role in the process. For this, at bottom, is what the controversy is or at least ought to be all about.

If the argument goes along at the same level as today, if the AFL-CIO, AIFLD, and the involved U.S. government agencies continue on their present course it is difficult to see how Jáuregui, tireless and able as he is, will successfully achieve his goal. The task of trying to move forward with an inter-American organization whose *latino* affiliates are mainly older, urban-centered types, closely influenced, if not controlled by government, presents enough difficulties. When in addition the ORIT leader is hobbled by a Yankee membership whose sincere belief that fighting communism is paramount to securing free trade unionism has unwittingly sustained the status quo in Latin America or abetted new undemocratic regimes; when, moreover, some Americans have really little respect for the ORIT, then Jáuregui's task is impossible. Under such conditions it might be better if Jáuregui took advantage of the AFL-CIO's withdrawal from the international ICFTU some years past and requested that the Americans also leave the ORIT, the Western Hemisphere affiliate of the ICFTU.[13]

Has the ORIT a future? There have been various speculations that the lessening of tensions between the major power blocs in the cold war will bring a decline of U.S. labor and U.S. government interest in ORIT with the consequent decline of that organization. Moreover, the question of the value that ORIT has been to the ordinary Latin American worker is one that repeatedly has been raised in recent years.[14] Furthermore, there is also what Jáuregui calls the unfriendly minority in the AFL-CIO. Under such circumstances the question may indeed be asked: Will ORIT be phased out?

Jáuregui insists that ORIT has a future, that "it is not a dying organization despite the AFL-CIO minority, and CLAT." Freed from the pressures of the cold war, which given the nature of its membership was bound to affect ORIT, the organization will according to Jáuregui intensify its concern with Latin American happenings. It will try to consumate the old dream of land reforms. In this matter it will not listen to voices in Washington that are disturbed by fears that land reform is really another means of abetting communism. It will identify itself even more firmly with the new popular nationalism. This is where the emphasis will go in building democratic trade unionism. In this new stance Jáuregui hopes that he will have the understanding of the U.S. government and U.S. labor. Understanding and technical assistance is what he hopes for from his friends among the *yanquis*. If that is not forthcoming, "we will go on without our American friends."

To Jáuregui, despite various critics, ORIT has justified its existence to Latin American workers and will continue to do so. Justified it, he insists, by fighting for free trade unionism throughout the hemisphere. It will continue the task of bringing to the Latin American workers the knowledge of free trade unionism. It will continue to organize unions, educate the workers in trade union practices, and persist in the long and complex journey towards constructing democratic unionism.

In its making trade unionism above all else its primary concern, Jáuregui argues ORIT is superior to CLAT. CLAT, like CLASC before it, he says, is a multipurposed body. Never really being a trade union movement the rival group, in whatever form, has played and continues to play a double game. It poses as a trade union body while it really is "a broker seeking votes." The very nature of CLAT reveals that it is not fundamentally interested in organizing and educating the unorganized workers.

The CLAT protagonists, of course, take a different view of the future. To them the new wider more embracing nature of their regional organization does not mean that they are less interested in trade unions. Since most of the workers in Latin America are unorganized, CLAT is making its appeal to all workers— organized or not. It is, to its protagonists, a workers movement in the broadest sense. It seeks contacts with all of the manifold kinds of worker groupings in Latin America which are deeply committed to change. ORIT, by contrast, is a tool of the Americans. Jáuregui may now be putting on a new face, but it is too late. He has been left behind by history. The masses of the workers will not be fooled. They will turn more and more to the organization that always has represented the interests of the poor workers, the organization that came to give them a meaningful choice between the Communists and the U.S.-Latin American "establishment" combination represented by ORIT.

Thus, the conflict continues. Jáuregui's strength in this struggle lies in his record of unfailing devotion to ORIT, as one who is above all else a *latino*, who whatever his close relations with the *yanquis* keeps Latin American interests primarily in mind. To these assets must be added his enormous capacity for hard work, his sense of diplomacy, his administrative capacity. (All things considered he is by far the best administrator of the four men who have occupied the office of ORIT secretary general since its founding.) His main weakness is that he has tried to accomplish the "impossible." He has always had to satisfy all the affiliates of an autonomous inter-American organization. He has in one sense always been trapped—caught between the interests of his *latino* brethren and those of the more powerful and affluent Yankee members as to where the emphasis should be placed in carrying out ORIT's declared mission of building democratic unionism.

Máspero's assets lie in the indigenous nature of the organization he leads, a purely Latin American militant body, the more positive consequences resulting from his particular foreign supporters in comparison with those of his rival, and particularly in the ideological appeal of which he himself has been the chief designer. The ideology contains the fierce call to the exploited ones to rally and to win the victory over the established order. But it goes beyond being an appeal for social revolution to obtain badly needed and justly deserved material gains. It also embodies an ardent belief in democracy and moral purpose.

Máspero reinforces Latin pride in his confidence that a purely native workers organization can do the job. He argues convincingly that differences in the values and culture between the United States and Latin America make it necessary that an organization devoted to the main task—which must be the making of a better life for the Latin American masses—must be native. To these assets he brings his unbounded energies, which include his accomplishments as a moving orator. He is able to move men to action. The CLASC under Máspero gave a much greater impression of vigor and drive than it did in the years that the equally dedicated but less ebullient and less aggressive José Goldsack was its leader. Máspero's weaknesses rest with the connotations still associated with any person or organization with a history of any kind of relation to the Catholic Church, the limitations of the native groups that affiliate with his movement and, especially, the nature of his personality.

To be sure no objective person would ever accuse Máspero of leading a "confessional" labor movement. It is only too apparent that the trend already far underway in CLASC, as in the former world Christian labor movement (the IFCTU), the trend towards relinquishing any kind of religious connections, led to the secularization expressed in CLASC's transformation into CLAT, which had followed IFCTU's transformation into the WCL. Yet such is the opposition to clericalism in Latin America (and elsewhere) that the suspicions still linger concerning CLAT and they must be daily confronted. As to the matter of the trade union following CLAT attracts, this has its positive and negative aspects. These unions are those more totally committed to change than those in ORIT. At the same time they are not as disciplined and organized as their rivals. They cannot look to the government to help, nor bargain with people who are more influential in Latin American societies and whose interests they more directly threaten than does ORIT.

Máspero's penchant for demagoguery at times cheapens the real worth of his ideology. His abrasive personality comes to the fore in these demagogic exhibitions which is all the more deplorable because he more than his rival has appreciated the need to answer the ideological impulse that is found in the *latino* worker. His flair for demagoguery, his conviction of his own rightness and suspicion of all who disagree have been noted inside the WCL circle as well as by those in the opposite camp. Of course, Máspero's frequently demagogic and aggressive manner may be a tactic which he feels brings the best payoff in arousing any audience to which he appeals. (Or it might be, as a scholarly Belgium priest, an ardent supporter of social change in Latin America, observed to the author, "Máspero.") Whatever his reasons Máspero's extreme attacks have supplied the most to the exchange of insults, innuendos, distortions, and mean deceits that have at times characterized his conflict with Arturo Jáuregui. It is ironic that Máspero, who by his emphasis upon the importance of ideology reveals that he more than his rival has understood the Latin American worker's receptivity to a gospel which clarifies the current situation and points in the direction of change, should by his cheap attacks also make the differences with Jáuregui appear as a personal feud and thus confuse the serious nature of the dispute.

At bottom, no matter what else the conflict is, or to what degree it makes an impact upon the workers, the dispute reflects different roads to change in Latin America. One (which Jáuregui follows) is to work for change by staying essentially within the system. The other (that of Máspero) indicates an essential despair of really accomplishing meaningful change through the current political system. If Jáuregui's style of leadership is less personalistic and less dynamically attractive to the understandably impatient seekers of extreme change, it is, nevertheless, relevant to the Latin American political scene. It demands skills and capabilities of a high order because it really avows that it will transcend the system by working within it. It is no less deserving of praise than the more militant ardent social revolutionary approach of the charismatic Máspero. This book ends with a tribute to both of the protagonists. May U.S. government, business, and labor elites by their future actions help create an ambient so that the conflict described here may continue within a compass that will be helpful to the Latin Americans. Such an atmosphere would, incidentally, contribute to the welfare of all Americans.

Appendix

Appendix

Before listing some "observations" concerning Arturo Jáuregui and Emilio Máspero which it is hoped will add a bit of human flavor to this study a brief account of how, where and when, the information here, and in the body of the book was gathered, may be helpful to the reader. The author took his training in political science just before the behavioral-statistical-scientific upsurge came upon the scene. He is a social scientist with a humanistic bent, and a former newspaper man. While he believes that there is such a specialized knowledge as the science of politics, he also believes that the term must be used with caution, and even somewhat loosely. There are many intelligent ways to the study of political problems and reasonable, intelligent men and women in the profession approach such problems more inclined to follow one path than another. The "how" of the gathering of the data in this book thus reflects the strengths and weaknesses of a dependency on countless interviews, some correspondence, omniverous reading in English and Spanish in a wide variety of sources, and much of what was called in the old newspaper world, "leg-work." It is only fair to tell the reader that while the author is a social scientist who, in gathering his information drew constantly, when the situation seemed appropriate, upon his knowledge of literature, poetry, music and theater, that he did not use a single questionnaire (refined or unrefined), or any of the other methods or tools of the ultra-modern political scientist. As was mentioned above one approaches political problems in different ways, using different tools.

The research for this study began in the late summer of 1966 when I went to Santiago, Chile where the headquarters of the CLASC was then located. Due to unforeseen circumstances the research continued more or less intermittently until the end of December 1972 when the last field work was completed in Mexico City. During these years the information was gathered on three continents. In Latin America I worked mainly in Santiago and Buenos Aires, Mexico City and Cuernavaca, Mexico. My Santiago and B.A. sojourns were from early September 1966 until the end of that year. Three months of that time was spent in Santiago with brief trips to Valparaiso. Subsequently I have spent some of my summer and Christmas vacation time working in Mexico. The summers of 1967, 1968, and 1970 were spent in Europe and most of the time was devoted to the research for this study. Bonn, Brussels, Geneva were my principle research locales, but other European cities, both on the continent and in Great Britain, were also visited. My other field study was done in Washington, D.C.

In the "Acknowledgments" I have indicated in a general way the many people to whom I am in one fashion or other indebted. Perhaps it may further assist the reader if I elaborate here a little more on the sources of the data. In Latin America I have visited and/or worked in the following centers: The central headquarters of the CLASC in Santiago; the Center of Research and Social

Action, of the Centro Bellarmino, also located in Santiago; the Di Tella institute, and the central headquarters of the trade union Light and Power, in Buenos Aires; the central headquarters of the ORIT, and of the FAT in Mexico City, as well as the ORIT Labor Institute in Cuernavaca, Mexico. In Europe I worked and/or visited the offices of the then IFCTU (now the WCL) and its rival the ICFTU, both of which are located in Brussels. A good part of two separate summers was spent in Geneva researching at the International Labor Office and in the headquarters of several union international secretariats. In Bonn I visited the offices of officials of two rival *stifdungen* as well as those of high level Germany clergy. Perhaps I should add the several days spent at the University of Louvain in Belgium talking to knowledgeable priests. In Washington, D.C., the headquarters of the AFL-CIO, the AIFLD and the "rival" UAW, were the sites of many interviews and the sifting over of written materials.

To indicate all these sources and to date the time period during which the information was gathered, fails to include several other sites and many other people that are part of the total research picture. The list of U.S. and foreign government officials, Latin American, European and American labor officials, political party leaders and functionaries, insightful clergymen, (especially "little" priests) I have talked, walked, eaten and drank with, in the course of this particular adventure, would fill several pages. These people, for one reason or other preferred to remain anonymous. As a former old-time newspaper man, I will always honor their requests. But they are remembered with gratitude.

Some Observations on the
Respective Leaders
Gathered Over the Years

Arturo Jáuregui

"Jáuregui is much more diplomatic than Máspero. He is pro-U.S., but he has at times been guilty of bad judgment. His greatest asset is his devotion to hard work something that his two predecessors in the Secretary Generalship of ORIT lacked. Jáuregui was always seeking to replace Luis Alberto Mongé, a deeper intellect, and he finally did." (A. U.S. European Mission Chief.)

"Fundamentally, Jáuregui is a Meany-Lovestone man, despite his real disagreements with some of the AFL-CIO or AIFLD hierarchy. He may even provoke minor quarrels with the Americans so as to give an appearance of independence. He is not as intellectually deep as Mongé who was more independent of the powerful Americans." (Canadian labor leader, emphatically pro-Reuther and anti-Meany.)

"Jáuregui is limited in his independence because ORIT is U.S. controlled. In his position he will always stand in the middle in the Reuther-Meany conflict. The only American in the ORIT secretariat that Jáuregui really liked was Morris Palidino. Most Americans are always telling Jáuregui that 'Mr. Meany says this and this.' George Meany probably doesn't know what is going on and Jay Lovestone is not too interested in Latin America." (A former U.S. labor attaché many years in Latin American posts.)

"Jáuregui has a working style that appeals to Americans but some of his predecessors also worked in a Latin American style and got things done. Jáuregui may talk about Máspero's flirtations with the Argentinian CGT but he himself also tries to woo the CGT." (Former CIO labor official, now European-based as an I.T.S. official.)

"Jáuregui is intelligent, hardworking, very smooth and clever. He probably would like to see less influence from the AFL-CIO in the ORIT but the Americans are in too many ways essential to financing the ORIT. Jáuregui tries to take a middle position between the Americans and the *latinos* in his organization. This most often pleases neither group and weakens the ORIT before Latin America." (An English I.L.O. specialist on Latin America.)

"Jáuregui is an intelligent, experienced, smooth labor bureaucrat who has sold out to George Meany. It is a pity that this intelligent man should betray his own people." (A high WCL official located in Brussels.)

105

"Jáuregui is an experienced labor leader and honest person but he is not a free man, being too dependent upon the Americans. It would be better for him and the ORIT if Jáuregui could have a more independent position." (A Belgian socialist, former labor official. A highly regarded figure of ICFTU circles.)

"Jáuregui is an experienced labor official. He is far more experienced and capable than Emilio Máspero. Máspero was never able to advance within the Argentine labor movement." (A high official of a prominent Argentinian confederation and former high official in the CGT.)

"Jáuregui is more temperate and sophisticated than Máspero, but he is not the kind of leader Latin America needs today for he is too compromised by his connections with the United States and the Latin American governments which the leaders of the big ORIT affiliates support." (A conservative French Christian labor spokesman.)

"Jáuregui is a good labor bureaucrat in the best sense of the word. He is not a revolutionist or ideologist. He has had his troubles with the AFL-CIO. Máspero by comparison is too extreme and too emotional. He is a ferverish revolutionary and ideologist." (A Latin American ex-ORIT high official.)

"Jáuregui is a good labor leader, but he leads an organization that talks revolution while accommodating to conservative governments all over Latin America." (A pro-CLAT peasant confederation official.)

"Arturo Jáuregui is one of the few genuinely honest trade union leaders in an area of the world that numbers a bare handful." (An American labor attaché and experienced Latin Americanist.)

"Jáuregui is a much more experienced labor leader than Máspero. He would be happier if he did not have to be so dependent upon the Americans in the ORIT for financial aid. He tries to assert the Latin feelings as much as possible while he works with George Meany and Jay Lovestone." (A Belgian socialist leader and labor specialist.)

"Jáuregui is the best of the ORIT secretary generals to date. He makes some efforts to achieve an independence from the AFL-CIO but he is really helpless since he is largely dependent upon the Americans for financial and technical assistance." (A U.S. Department of State labor specialist.)

"Jáuregui is a diplomat, but his diplomacy is always, in the end, suited to advance George Meany's ends. He knows that his bread is buttered by Meany and Lovestone." (An ILO pro-WCL official of long experience in the French and German labor movements.)

Emilio Máspero

"When Máspero raises his voice and pounds the desk it is necessary to also pound the desk. Too few CLASC people can do this. But there are some who, while they respect him, can tell him to go to hell when they don't agree. To really get along with Máspero you have to be able on occasion to tell him to go to hell." (A European, and former high IFCTU official.)

"He is dogmatic, multi-argumentative—a typical Argentinian nationalist. You get seasick trying to argue with him. He is too extreme in his condemnation of the U.S. He lacks a historical sense in his present anti-U.S. attitude." (A Chilean lawyer [Christian Democrat], labor specialist, and former CLASC official.)

"Máspero is certainly no diplomat, but he is the best contemporary labor leader in Latin America. It is unfortunate that Máspero is practically the only outstanding figure and strong character in the CLASC to the present time, but such is the case and under his guidance the CLASC is progressing." (A former IFCTU [now WCL] official.)

"Máspero is a ruthless fighter and vigorous leader. His predecessor José Goldsack will remain and play a positive role in his quiet way within CLASC in Chile. He is bitter about Máspero's rough tactics, but he is a more loyal organization man that Máspero would be if the circumstances were reversed. There is no doubt, however, that Máspero is the leader of the Latin American Christian unionists." (An ILO labor specialist, sympathetic to left-wing Christian labor.)

"Máspero is bright but he is not wise in many of his actions. A shrewd critic of ORIT's weaknesses, however. He seeks to dominate and control everything." (A British labor attaché of long Latin American experience.)

"Máspero has much at stake and might be leery of talking for a professor's benefit. But he must (and he has) taken criticism from his fellow officials within the CLASC." (A CLASC peasant union leader.)

"He is an arrogant leader of an insignificant group. He is blatantly anti-American yet has the nerve to complain that American embassies in Latin America don't help him. If he came to me, I'd help him—to the door." (A veteran U.S. labor attaché.)

"Máspero is impetuous, but brilliant. He is ruthless and showed it in the way he went after José Goldsack's job. I do not care for him personally but as long as he is the chosen leader of CLASC I will follow him. He must be really getting to Jáuregui and his American cohorts for they cannot ignore him as they would prefer to. He is our good weapon." (A Chilean Christian Democrat intellectual.)

"Máspero claims that the CLASC built this union. I am a Christian Democrat but neither the Christian Democrat party nor the CLASC built our union. The *campesinos* who accepted my leadership were responsible for our union. We suffered and worked together and now Máspero says it was CLASC that did the work." (A Chilean leader of an important peasant Christian union.)

"Máspero is brilliant. He is by far the most knowledgeable of the Christian Latin American trade unionists. I think his excessive anti-Americanism will lessen as he lives with the responsibilities of his office." (A Belgian Christian Trade Union official.)

"Máspero is a 'prophet' who egotistically views himself as the great leader of the Latin American workers. He has a facile mind and is loaded with ideas but he is a poor organizer. He 'talks' Christian trade unionism but most of his actual unions are merely on paper. In his early days in Argentina he was a *Peronista*." (A conservative European Christian labor specialist and student of Latin America.)

"Máspero is a totalitarian extremist. Reportedly when he first entered the CLASC picture in Chile he told Father Vekemans that he would try to fuse the Christians with the Argentine Peronistas." (An experienced American labor attaché in Latin American affairs.)

"Máspero is the dynamic outstanding leader of the CLASC, but CLASC is much more than Máspero and should not be identified solely with him." (A Chilean Jesuit experienced in labor politics.)

"Máspero is a highly 'personalist' leader—like Castro. He suspects or opposes those who do not agree with him. Too negative, too 'anti' in his views—anti-U.S., anti-church, etc. However, he is our elected leader and must be accepted as U.S. Democrats accepted L.B.J." (A Chilean Christian Democrat of the Frei faction.)

"Máspero is the best man for the job, but he needs guidance. Strong-willed and at times, too demagogic and anti-American he is learning now that he is the secretary general to curb his demagoguery and his too extreme anti-Yankeeism. He is changing. This will make him all the more effective in his praiseworthy task of opposing the American trade union image that the Americans seek to impose on Latin America." (A former Christian trade union high official at the central office in Brussels.)

"Máspero is a brilliant, highly emotional person, a typical assertive Argentine nationalist. He hasn't changed since taking office and it is very doubtful if he ever will." (A Belgium priest and Latin American specialist of many years.)

"Máspero is highly intelligent. A powerful orator he has a great ability in moving audiences and making people feel that they agree with him—whether they actually do so or not. He is very impressive and convincing yet he is also deeply emotional, dogmatic and basically anti-America." (An American director of an American business research foundation in Latin America.)

"Máspero is a difficult person, an unpleasant and irritating individual, but a dynamic and aggressive man. He is the man for the job at this stage of the CLASC's development. A capable labor leader." (A leader of the Christian Democrats in Mexico.)

Notes

Notes

Chapter 1

1. Both Jáuregui and Máspero oppose revolution which in seeking avowedly praiseworthy ends finds it necessary to repudiate democratic means. Their reflections on Communist revolutions avowedly made in the people's interest are indicated below.

2. Several studies have indicated this mainly "U.S. versus Europe" support of the ORIT and the CLASC respectively. For two examples, see Gladys Delmas, "Labor's Alarming Christians," REPORTER, February 25, 1965, pp. 27-30, and Henry A. Landsberger, "International Labor Organization," in INTEGRATION OF MAN AND SOCIETY IN LATIN AMERICA, Samuel Shapiro, ed., Notre Dame, Indiana, 1967.

3. I would agree with Landsberger (cf., footnote 2) that the foreign sums at the disposal of the CLASC are probably smaller than those of the ORIT's outside benefactors, but that what is important is that the sources are from outside Latin America.

4. U.S. government funds, from AID of the Department of State and funds from American business plus AFL-CIO money support may be channelized through the American Institute for Free Labor Development, located in Washington, D.C. The AIFLD has operated throughout Latin America as an educational and social projects agency. The major share of its budget is paid by the AID. It is controlled by its labor representatives and bears the imprint and blessing of George Meany, AFL-CIO president, and his numerous supporters in that organization. The United Automobile Workers, however, who were expelled from the AFL-CIO in 1968, are long-time critics of the AIFLD.

5. Whether all this, however, justifies the assertion that the source of funds of the AIFLD constitutes a source for the ORIT (and that, therefore, U.S. business money and government funds eventually comes to the ORIT treasury) is conjectural. Ironically, the AIFLD is in some respects, notably in workers' education, a rival of the ORIT. The AIFLD is in some ways a competitor throughout Latin America with the ORIT. A helpful study of the activities of the AFL-CIO in Latin America and its relations with U.S. government and American corporations is that prepared for the Senate Subcommittee on American Republics Affairs, July 15, 1968, 90th Congress, 2nd Session (Washington, D.C.: U.S. Government Printing Office, 1968). The contributions from all affiliates of the ORIT can be found in INFORME SEPTIMO CONGRESSO (Cuernavaca, Mexico: Marzo, 1970).

6. I have been told repeatedly that European labor leaders have for the most part regarded Latin America as a special province of the AFL-CIO. One British labor attaché, commenting on the British Trade Union Congress' general

indifference to foreign affairs and this laxity within the ICFTU, remarked that George Woodcock, then the TUC's most important leader, regards Latin America as "Meany's territory." Some European labor leaders affiliated with the ICFTU (particularly the Scandinavians), were, however, interested in exerting an influence in that organization's Latin American policies. They were not content to write off Latin America as "Meany's territory."

7. Konrad Adenauer group's opposite number is the Frederich Ebert *Stifdung* whose labor adherents are affiliated with the ICFTU, to which the ORIT also belongs. According to a conversation I had with a representative (a German) of the Konrad Adenauer *Stifdung* in Mexico City, in January 1968, the Frederich Ebert *Stifdung*, under the auspices of the German government, was being brought into closer cooperation with its Christian counterpart. He felt that in the future the K.A. *Stifdung* would have the more dominant role in Latin America. It may be assumed that the financial assistance which either of these two foundations receive from their government rises and falls with the success or failure of the rival parties, the Socialists and the Christian Democrats.

8. Professor Henry A. Landsberger, formerly of the New York State School of Industrial and Labor Relations, Cornell University, has pointed out that these rivals are, "to an important degree, not Latin American." Cf. "International Labor Organizations," op. cit. For the United States and European influences upon these two contestants see also Robert Alexander, ORGANIZED LABOR IN LATIN AMERICA, New York, 1965, pp. 248-51, 253-54, 257, and pp. 259-60.

9. The young Máspero's experience in the novitiate is regularly brought up when one is conversing with his friends and critics inside Christian labor circles. To his admirers it presumably contributed to the brilliance, the driving force in presenting his beliefs, the sense of mission, that one experiences in talking with him. Conversely one of the most scholarly priests in Latin America, himself a Jesuit, remarking that the CLASC leader was a "brilliant" but not a "wise man," added that Máspero's interrupted experience in the novitiate and other contacts with the Order of the Society of Jesus, had contributed to making him a "half-baked Jesuit."

10. The J.O.C. itself played an important role in the creation of Christian trade union groups throughout Latin America in the years before 1954. It was out of the activities of these generally small Christian worker groupings that the CLASC was later to emerge.

11. The taint of *Peronismo* is something that Máspero himself has had to contend with to this day. To his opponents, principally of the ORIT and their supporters (including some U.S. labor attachés), Máspero was an early *Peronista* who continues to reveal the characteristics of the authoritarian, anti-capitalism *justicialismo*, the **Peronist** ideology. A leading Latin American supporter of CLASC who, while critical of Máspero, agreed that as the duly elected Christian labor leader, he must be supported, characterized Máspero, "as an ex-Peronista

has totalitarian tendencies." Contrarywise, I have repeatedly also heard expressed both inside and outside of the Christian circles the view given me by a famous Argentine economist, a balanced critic of both CLASC and ORIT, that Máspero during his time as a very young metal worker was a leading member of ASA, "itself of little importance in the Argentine labor scene" and "of the pro-Christian, *anti-Peronista* minority." In an interview I had with him Nov. 2, 1966, in Santiago, Máspero was highly critical of Peron's totalitarianism.

12. José Rangel Parra, Venezuelan *campesino* leader who is the present secretary general of CLASC's peasant federation, FCL, and other leaders of the CLASC have stayed with Máspero over the years. This, however, does not mean that they are in any sense his compliant servers. Indeed, there are some of them who have the ability to tell their leaders off in blunt language, a necessary requirement I was told by one of the highest figures in the Christian labor world for effectively dealing with Emilio Máspero. The "decent man"–José Goldsack, in contrast, is not of such temperament and this played some part in his demise as CLASC's leader. Several of his friends who felt that the aggressive Máspero was bound to replace him, nevertheless were unhappy that "Pepe" (Goldsack) did not go down fighting.

13. A mutual friend mentioned that Jáuregui once told him that almost from the time that Jáuregui learned to read, he devoured many classics while his friends and schoolmates were thinking of little more than *futbol.*

14. Jáuregui remains an *Aprista* to this day despite the subsequent recent checkered maneuverings of the party which among other things brought it into a political front with its old enemies in Peru. As an *Aprista* he has come to accept the less extreme revolutionary views that now characterize the movement in contrast to its earlier program.

15. In addition, the ORIT soon also acquired as affiliates the CIO and the Canadian Congress of Labor, and some of the Latin American confederations which had remained with the WFTU until its division. Most important of these was the *Confederación de Trabajadores Mexicanos* (CTM). The CTM, which had withdrawn from the founding convention in protest over the ORIT's refusal to admit the Argentinean CGT, rejoined the ORIT early in 1953.

16. These, in addition to Jáuregui have been in chronological order, Francisco Aguirre of Cuba, the Costa Rican Luis Alberto Mongé, and Alfonso Sanchez Madariaga of Mexico. The continuing ingrained antipathy toward communism on the part of the ORIT leader was again illustrated in the spring of 1970 when Máspero personally visited Jáuregui to try to interest him in one of Máspero's favorite goals, that of creating a new hemispheric *latino* labor organization that might include Communists who accepted its principles. Jáuregui, mindful of his experiences with Communists, rejected Máspero's plan. He took a rather dim view of the November 1970 meeting of CLASC leaders and Communists with the newly created Chilean president, socialist Salvador Allende, and the CUTCH leaders. (CUTCH is the national trade union organization

in Chile which for years has had a majority of Socialists and Communists in its leadership.) It is characteristic of Jáuregui that, following his usual custom where elected presidents in Latin American countries are not avowed subscribers to totalitarian philosophies, he sent Allende a telegram congratulating the Chilean socialist leader on his election. Jáuregui feels that the December 1970 meeting of an "Andes Group," the CLASC and Communist representative in South America, to push forward with plans for unity only underscores the correctness of his refusal to accept the earlier Máspero proposals to him. The Communists, ever since the expiration years ago of the CTAL mainly as the result of the ORIT offensives, have had a Permanent Congress for Trade Union Unity of the workers of Latin America, (CPUSTAL), closely affiliated with the Communist-oriented WFTU. This body has been, as Jáuregui well knows, seeking to get some kind of regional successor to the CTAL. Its line has been one of labor unity. CPUSTAL has had several meetings and made several agreements in different Latin American countries with CLASC concerning joint efforts to seek unity. These have been acknowledged by the WFTU Secretariat. Jáuregui, aware of this, will not accept a proposal of unity which he regards as an aid to forwarding Communist-approved ends.

Chapter 2

1. Aware that the countryside has been neglected by trade unions, both Máspero and Jáuregui in recent years, in actual efforts at organization and in educational and propaganda programs, as well as in hemispheric meetings and congresses, have endeavored to make up for past neglect. It must be noted that CLASC had a greater attractiveness in its more militant message for the peasant movements and this militancy now is part of the CLAT. The ORIT in its past approach was somewhat limited by being an organization with which the urban, more traditional type of unions are found. But the ORIT, also, has increased its organizational, educational, and propaganda activities aimed at attracting the peasantry.

2. For a description of the ideal patterns common throughout Latin America and their origins, see Charles Wagley, THE LATIN AMERICAN TRADITION, New York and London, 1969, pp. 3 ff. On what he calls the "history of accommodation" see Victor Alba, ALLIANCE WITHOUT ALLIES, New York, 1965, pp. 99-108.

3. The reader is reminded that the picture of Latin America presented here for background purposes is a general one. Conditions vary in the different countries. For example in some countries, such as Chile, there is a significant militancy and challenge to the social order expressed in the ideology of the national labor confederations. But, the overall picture of trade unionism is the one that has been given here. And this, despite differences which do exist, also

applies to such things as education, sources of income, social status, and politics, throughout Latin America.

Chapter 3

1. In the last few years the ORIT, mindful of the special efforts of the CLASC (now CLAT) in the agrarian sectors, has stepped up its activities concerning peasant trade unionism. Since 1967 a yearly inter-American seminar dealing with problems of *campesinos* has been sponsored by the ORIT. The 1969 session was devoted to the special problems of *campesino* leaders. In January 1971 a special two-weeks seminar devoted to ideology and the peasantry was held at Cuernavaca.

2. Conversation with the author.

3. TWENTY YEARS OF FREE TRADE UNIONISM IN AMERICA (Mexico: Impresiones Modernas, 1971(?)), p. 65.

4. Ibid., p. 66.

5. Ibid., pp. 58-64 passim. On page 60 is the following statement:

The economic and political groups committed to international capitalism have used all the means at their disposal to impede the access to power of the popular parties with true Latin American roots, deforming their ideology and promoting their infiltration by persons who have betrayed the possibilities of creating an Indo-American political philosophy and mentality which would unify us politically and economically. The hemispheric organizations created for this purpose have not been able to do this, because they are emasculated by compromised officials, obsequious politicians and technicians most of who deform reality because they, too, serve other interests.

6. Ibid., p. 102.

7. Ibid., p. 103.

8. Ibid., pp. 80-85, 128-35 passim.

9. Ibid., p. 134.

10. Ibid., p. 135. It should be noted that Armando Gonzales like the other delegates quoted here was highly critical of Social-Christianism and CLASC who far from regarding as revolutionaries they viewed as practitioners of revamped techniques to subjugate the masses in the interests of the Church.

11. Ibid., pp. 137-41 passim.

12. EL DIA (Mexico City) July 4, 1969. Jáuregui is quoted in an article from Brussels by Marcel Baufrere which deals with the ORIT leader's reactions to various questions concerning ORIT's position in the world labor picture. (Translation from Spanish by the author.)

13. EL DIA, ibid.

14. The CLASC since its founding, partly because the neglected agrarian sector offered a greater opportunity for organization, put a good deal of effort into bringing its message to the countryside. It has sponsored the regional

Federacion Campesina Latina Americana (FCL) through which it seeks to spread its influence throughout the area. Credit must be given to CLASC for originally taking the initiative in the task of organizing the peasants. This task has also reflected internal problems within the CLASC. Some leaders of viable peasant unions, Hector Alarcon for example, resented Máspero's tactics and have gone their own ways. The FCL leaders today, however, are in accord with Máspero.

15. All of this is in keeping with the increasing democratic radicalization and secularization that has been manifest in recent years which was earlier reflected in the divisions within the Christian trade union movement. The French Christian unions originally most forcibly illustrated this division and it terminated with the radicals leaving to form their own union in which the name "Christian" was dropped. The continuing more radical bent is shown in the changing of the name of the International Federation of Christian Trade Unions, the Christian world labor body which had its origins in the anti-socialist and confessional Catholic supported grouping of the early twentieth century. In the fall of 1968, the sixteenth worldwide Congress of the IFCTU changed its name to the World Confederation of Labor. The CLASC (now CLAT), like the IFCTU (now WCL), stands to the political left of the ORIT and its "parent" body, the International Confederation of Free Trade Unions (ICFTU). At the Caracas Congress which transformed the CLASC into the CLAT the WCL was represented by its deputy general secretary, Carlos Custer, among others. Subsequently he and the general secretary of the WCL, Jean Bruck, have participated in the meetings of the Executive Committee of the CLAT in which the resolutions of the November 1971 Congress were discussed. Carlos Custer also has represented the WCL at the FAT (Frente Autentics de Trabajo), the Mexican affiliate of CLAT, whose general secretary Alfredo Dominquez is a member of CLAT's Executive Committee that Emilio Máspero heads. Máspero thus was a major force in moving not only the CLASC but also the world labor organization, the WCL, along the new course. Cf. "The WCL Seen from Latin America," THE WCL: UNITY IN DIVERSITY (a special issue of LABOR, the WCL magazine Nrs. 3-4, 1970), Brussels. Also see ALGUNOS APUNTES PARA SEGUIR A UNA PRIMERA DISCUSION SOBRE LA ESTRATEGIA, LA POLITICA, Y EL PROGRAMA DE ACCION DE LA C.M.T., XVII CONGRESO Gienbra, 28-31 Mayo 1969, and PODER SINDICAL, Febrero 1969, Fondo Latino American De Cullura Popular. The resolutions of the "transforming" Congress are embodied in three mimeographed volumes published by the CLAT headquarters at Caracas.

16. The source is LABOR, No. 5, 1968, pp. 193-202. (Italics in the original.)

17. Cf. Emilio Máspero, "Trade Unionism as an Instrument of the Latin American Revolution," in LATIN AMERICAN RADICALISM, Horowitz, de Castro, and Gerassi, eds. (New York: Vintage Books, 1969), pp. 207-208.

18. Ibid., p. 208. (Italics in the original.)

19. CLASC, (English edition), Year 1, Number 7, July 1969, p. 3.

20. This exposition of Máspero's view of the class struggle, its implications and consequences, is found in EL PAPEL DE LOS TRABAJADORES EN LA CONSTRUCTION DEL SOCIALISMO COMUNITARIO, Merida Venezuela, Julio 16 al 21 de 1972, pp. 12-16.

21. The sources for these views on clericalism and religion are ibid., pp. 32-36, and VI CONGRESSO LATINO AMERICANO DE TRABAJADORES, 21 al 27 de Novembre de 1971, pp. 37-39.

Chapter 4

1. THE INTER-AMERICAN LABOR BULLETIN, January-February 1964, p. 3. Jáuregui is emphatic that his fundamentally friendly view of the United States is in no sense one of being subservient to the "big neighbor." During many years of knowing him I have heard him repeatedly state, "We are nobody's colonials."

2. "We are no loudspeaker for the economic and political ideas of any particular country. We do disseminate the ideas of any member affiliate but we do not enforce any particular country's viewpoint. The ORIT Executive Board represents different points of view—capitalism and socialism in varying degrees." Interview, Mexico City, December 1967. Five years later in another interview he said, "I have never believed in old or new capitalism as a system. I do believe in the need for capital for investment in joint honest work."

3. Perhaps the best summary of Jáuregui's attitude and role concerning the United States which reveals his delicate problem as one who must in his position "walk a tight-rope" is that made to me by a Mexican jurist. Commenting that it is through the ORIT that the United States has one of its few open doors to Latin America he pointed out that this entree is mainly due to Jáuregui who has insisted on a relationship based on mutual respect. He added "Jáuregui is the only man in the ORIT who can handle its Latin American members. His enemies charge that he has made them the captives of the United States. But they do not realize that the Latin American members respect Jáuregui and know that he is first of all a *latino* who is no tool of the United States. Among these members are Latin American leaders of labor who are themselves, for the most part, independent-minded in their attitudes towards your country."

4. RELIGION, REVOLUTION AND REFORM, William V. D'Antonio and Frederick B. Pike, (eds.), New York, 1964, p. 173. (On the same page Máspero states that in the United States capitalism "has shown itself capable of improving the lives of the laboring masses.") He has reservations concerning the AFL-CIO view that capitalism is necessary to free trade unionism and essential to democracy. Concerning free trade unionism and capitalism's necessary relationship he writes, "This statement appears to be applicable within the North

American context, even though I might not subscribe to it totally were I a North American."

5. "Democracy has many times been confused with capitalism, as if the capitalist system were essential to democracy." He goes on to indicate that in "Latin America the penchant to picture capitalism and democracy as bedfellows has caused many to lose hope in political freedom, to reject democracy, and to incline towards totalitarianism." William V. D'Antonio and Frederick B. Pike, op. cit., pp. 173-74.

6. Interview, Mexico City, January 1968. Jáuregui earlier had been a principal figure in shaping the resolution of the second ORIT regional conference on Labor Education, held in Cuernavaca, Mexico, in January 1967. This resolution asserted labor's desire for a meaningful role in Alpro's policy-making decisions.

7. Conversation with Joseph J. Palisi, former editor of the AIFLD RE-PORT, a monthly organ of the American Institute for Free Labor Development, January 1968, at the Catholic Inter-American Cooperative (CICOP) annual convention in St. Louis. Mr. Palisi resigned his position with AIFLD in June 1966. He subsequently became an open critic of the AIFLD. His writings concerning the rivalry between ORIT and CLASC, and the ideology of the CLASC, have been circulated by the CLASC.

8. Cf. D'Antonio and Pike, op. cit., p. 239.

9. Jáuregui's attitude specifically with regard to the Cuban and Dominican interventions are discussed below.

10. The *Confederación de Trabajadores de America Latina* (CTAL) founded in 1936 as an organization of various left and liberal elements of Latin American labor. In the years after World War II it steadily passed into pro-Communist hands. The brilliant Mexican Marxist, Vincente Lombardo Toledano, headed the CTAL. Not a Communist, he was closely identified with the pro-Communist position. He was a vice-president of the WFTU, the Soviet approved international labor body. The CTAL was the Western Hemisphere's affiliate of the WFTU.

11. Specifically in this regard Jáuregui cites the ORIT's messages to the Brazilian military junta which overthrew the Goulart administration in April 1964. Since the downfall of Goulart, however, Brazilian labor's right to seek its own destiny has not been respected by the junta forces which overthrew Goulart and have controlled Brazil ever since. In passing it should be noted that the AFL-CIO's critical attitude toward Goulart along with that of the AIFLD once again brought forth the charge that the ORIT's similar position was dictated by its close relationship to Yankee labor and to Washington. Washington had quickly recognized the new regime in Brazil, sending it its warmest wishes (NEW YORK TIMES, April 3, 1964, p. 1). Jáuregui's view of the matter is that he and the ORIT have always stood for a free labor movement in Brazil. When President Goulart, who had Communist support, was overthrown, the ORIT, as indicated,

reminded those who succeeded him of this position. And the ORIT, according to Jáuregui, has continued to remind the subsequent authoritarian rulers of the revolutionary Brazilian regime of its belief in unfettered trade unionism.

12. "Negative anti-communism often associated simply with blind opposition to change is habitually fostered by American foreign policy" (D'Antonio and Pike, op. cit., p. 173). Máspero incidentally was critical of the positions taken by Washington and by the ORIT concerning the overthrow of Goulart in Brazil. A major concern of the U.S. government and the AFL-CIO at the time was what they saw as the increasing pro-Communist Goulart actions.

13. Jáuregui was a long-time intimate friend of Serafino Romualdi, the former AFL-CIO Latin American representative of many years. Romualdi frequently expressed his great admiration for Jáuregui as a loyal, efficient ORIT administrator and a Latin American democratic labor leader. It is fair, therefore, to conclude that among others Romualdi had Jáuregui in mind in writing about the prelude and aftermath of the U.S.-supported attack on Castro's Cuba in April 1961, as follows: "I must say emphatically, that I never met a Latin American labor, political or governmental leader or democratic affiliation who did not express to me the hope that the job would be done soon and well." Romualdi goes on to state that after the disastrous defeat he never encountered "any Latin American of democratic affiliation who expressed regret that we had helped the ill-fated Cuban invasions. The only regret that they expressed is that we did not go all the way and assume the victory of the enterprise." These quotations are from Romualdi's book, PRESIDENTS AND PEONS: RECOLLECTIONS OF A LABOR AMBASSADOR IN LATIN AMERICA (New York, 1967), Funk and Wagnalls, p. 224 and pp. 226-27. It should be noted that the only affiliate of the ORIT to censor the United States government for its part in the landing was the Canadian Congress of Labor. (Incidentally, concerning another matter years later, the Canadian affiliates' contribution paid for the construction of a library on the grounds of the ORIT's Cuernavaca school. Jáuregui likes to joke about this instance of "Canadian imperialism" replacing "Yankee imperialism." According to him a high CLASC official speaking in Canada to the CLASC affiliate there, denounced the CCL for aiding the ORIT school and in effect thus aiding Yankee imperialism. Naturally neither the ORIT, Canadians, or Jáuregui, see it in that light.)

14. INTER-AMERICAN LABOR BULLETIN, May 1965, p. 2.

15. Conversations with the author. The whole ORIT-Cuban history is a complicated one. Cuban labor leaders of the CTC had played a prominent role in the formation of the ORIT. ORIT's first secretary general, Francisco Aguirre, was a Cuban, and the controversial Eusebio Mujal, CTC chief and powerful Cuban labor leader, was a member of the first ORIT Executive Committee. Havana was the site of ORIT headquarters during the initial two years. The strategy and tactics of CTC, the ORIT's Cuban affiliate and especially the role of Mujal in its relationships with Fulgencio Batista and Fidel Castro in the years

prior to Batista's downfall and for a brief time after, had their repercussions in the controversies within the top circles of the ORIT itself. For differing views on all this see Romualdi, op. cit., Chapters 13-15, and Ronald Radosh, AMERICAN LABOR AND UNITED STATES FOREIGN POLICY, New York, 1969, pp. 375-82.

16. To some specialists CASC was the strongest labor grouping affiliated with the CLASC.

17. INTER-AMERICAN LABOR BULLETIN, July 1966, p. 3. The ORIT leader also likes to emphasize that in the case of the then newly elected president Dr. Joaquim Balaguer (as in similar cases in Latin America), he accompanied his congratulations on Balaguer's victory with the reminder that unrestricted exercise of trade union rights should be maintained in the Dominican Republic during the Balaguer administration.

18. Máspero's suspicions concerning the CIA affected the writer personally. After more than two months spent in doing research in Santiago, Chile, mainly at the CLASC headquarters, I was, on the basis of a letter received from a CLASC agent in Washington, D.C., declared by Máspero to be a possible CIA agent. This prevented me from going on to the new headquarters which was shifted to Caracas in December 1966. Subsequently the writer received cooperation from some CLASC officials in Mexico and from informed sympathizers with CLASC in that country. In the summers of 1967 and 1968 I received assistance from IFCTU officials in Belgium and Christian union sympathizers in Geneva. An important CLASC official, a Latin American, told me during my 1967 summer European trip that "Máspero still believes you to be a CIA agent." Again in December 1972, I found officers of the Mexican affiliate of the CLAT most cooperative as I traveled between them and their rivals at the ORIT headquarters discussing divergent views. The belief that I was employed by the CIA was once very politely explained to me in Chile by a CLASC high officer, also like Máspero an Argentinian, as based on the evidence that many sincere American professors think that being an agent is a way of honestly serving their country.

19. These overall impressions of the Máspero's leader's view concerning U.S. foreign policies were obtained in a lengthy interview before, during, and after lunch at his home in Santiago, Chile, in November 1966. In the course of the conversations, Máspero remarked that his attack upon U.S. imperialistic policies did not differ greatly from criticisms of U.S.-Latin American relations that President Kennedy and Senator J. William Fulbright had themselves expressed.

20. It is worth repeating that the CTC was a (if not *the*) principal Latin American labor organization in the founding of the ORIT in 1951. When certain affiliates in the ORIT sought years later to condemn CTC actions in support of Batista the attempt was successfully opposed by other affiliates including the AFL-CIO. The story of the CTC activities, however, in relation to Batista and the ORIT reactions to them, as well as the CTC-ORIT-Castro story in its origins, is, as I have said, a complex one.

21. Joseph J. Palisi, "A Brief Analysis of the Evolving Ideology of the CLASC," DEPTO, PRENSA CLASC, Agosto 1966, pp. 18-19.

22. This caveat as well as Article 6 of the Treaty of Rio de Janeiro of 1947 lay to hand for interpretation by the United States its AFL-CIO and ORIT defenders in explaining the presumed legality of U.S. intervention to preserve the Dominican Republic against the danger of Communist infiltration. The later meeting of the OAS after U.S. unilateral intervention which provided for an inter-American contingent of troops being dispatched to the Dominican Republic was also an additional helpful factor which could be used by those who defended the American action.

23. D'Antonio and Pike, op. cit., p. 239.

24. According to a former OAS labor official, who actively worked on the COSATE during these years, the CLASC while absenting itself from the Committee tried to gain OAS assistance through "their own Jesuit organizations." But these organizations were not genuine labor groups and thus could not receive OAS aid. (Conversations in Washington and Mexico.)

25. "Declaración del Consejo Ejecutivos de la ORIT Respecto al COSATE (OEA)," NOTICIARIO OBRERO INTERAMERICANO, Marzo 1968, p. 3.

Chapter 5

1. To quote Jáuregui in an interview with him in Mexico City in December 1972, "McClellan's judgment of me and of ORIT is a simple case of paranoia which I am not a specialist in healing." Jáuregui's attitude and actions towards the successor to Morris Palidino as assistant secretary general of the ORIT further indicates his independent attitude. Palidino, the American representative in the ORIT central office, had been greatly admired by Jáuregui. His successor, according to Jáuregui, fancied himself as George Meany's watchdog in the office, rather than Jáuregui's aide as an ORIT official. The upshot of the disagreement was that the person in question was transferred out of the ORIT office and that there was an understanding that the offices of assistant secretaries of ORIT would be void of representatives from U.S. labor for the indefinite future.

2. It must be clearly understood that whatever criticisms the ORIT leader makes of the AIFLD director William Doherty Jr., he has the greatest regard for Doherty as a friend and a high appreciation of the AIFLD director's administrative ability. Doherty is first of all a man with a good Latin American background having worked in the area for the PTTI (Postal, Telegraph and Telephone International), an international trade secretariat, before coming to the AIFLD. Jáuregui regards Doherty as a man very sensitive to *latino* feelings. He is *muy simpatico* a warm, open type of personality, happy family man— characteristics which appeal to Latin Americans. Jáuregui regards Doherty as a broadly educated man with an analytical mentality. All of these positive qualities in the AIFLD director the ORIT leader feels are in contrast with some

of the AFL-CIO figures who influence that organization's Latin American stance. But Jáuregui's admiration for his good friend Bill Doherty doesn't lessen his unhappiness with what he feels have been the actions of some of Doherty's country program directors which adversely affect American relations in Latin America and with the ORIT.

3. He mentioned the case of one graduate student who did come to the ORIT headquarters and was assisted in his investigations. When the researcher failed to find the evidence of ORIT's being the tool and financial dependent of the United States, he left. "He came to us with a preconceived image of what he wanted to find. We assisted him in every way. When he didn't discover that which *he* knew existed, he had no more interest in us." Jáuregui in an interview, December 1972.

4. For a critical view of AFL-CIO policies in Latin America see the U.S. Senate Committee on Foreign Relations, SURVEY OF THE ALLIANCE FOR PROGRESS, LABOR POLICIES AND PROGRAMS, 90th Congress, 2nd Session, July 15, 1968, passim. In one conversation concerning Jáuregui's relations with Meany and Lovestone, the ORIT leader told the writer that he got along well with them. "But," he added, "Washington is not Rome and neither George Meany nor Jay Lovestone are the pope." I always have had the impression that while Jáuregui respected the AFL-CIO president, he was at times irked by the constant concern of many American representatives in and out of the ORIT office for "what Mr. Meany thinks,"—with regard to matters relating to all the affiliates of the ORIT. A friend of Meany, Jáuregui also had a high regard for the late Walter Reuther, Meany's rival and critic within the American labor movement.

5. Máspero, EL PAPEL DE LOS TRABAJADORES EN LA CONSTRUC-TION DEL SOCIALISMO COMUNITARIO, Merida, Venezuela, Julio 16 al 21 de 1972, pp. 39-41.

6. The charge of confessionalism which periodically reappears reflects the lingering of an old suspicion. I have had numerous Latin American and European trade unionists, and even a few Americans, all either labor officials or close students of the world labor movement, indicate their reluctance to believe that CLASC was not in one fashion or other an instrument of the Catholic Church. A high member of the Belgium Socialist party, a labor leader of international reputation, once told me that "CLASC is not run by the Church in any formal sense, but its members are really controlled by the Church in the most effective fashion here." And he tapped his chest over the heart. The suspicion lingers on even with the change of CLASC to CLAT, despite Máspero's even more pointed attacks on clericalism of any kind. CLAT's opponents in the ORIT believe that there is an internal division within CLAT with certain affiliating groupings being very close to the Church.

Chapter 6

1. Staff of the Committee on Foreign Relations, United States Senate, SURVEY OF THE ALLIANCE FOR PROGRESS: LABOR POLICIES AND PROGRAMS, 90th Congress, 2nd Session, July 15, 1968 (Washington, D.C.: U.S. Government Printing Office, 1968).

2. See the examples of the "Workers Charter" of the First Union Conference on Latin American Development and Integration held in Santo Domingo in May, 1968, Máspero's notes for STRATEGY POLICY AND ACTIONS PROGRAM OF THE WCL, THE XVII CONGRESS OF THE WCL, cited (in Spanish), "The WCL seen from Latin America," cited, and especially, PODER SINDICAL.

3. Castro's Cuba is a suggestive lesson in this regard. Its totalitarian socialist order may be preferable to the Batista capitalist dictatorship, but it is not a democracy no matter what it is called by its partisans. It may be that conditions in most countries in Latin America are such as to really preclude the complete necessary renovation of societies while maintaining a fundamentally democratic new order. Máspero, it is assumed, belongs to those who believe that difficult as it may be such a new future can be made possible. He does not accept the Castro solution, the Peronista solution, nor the new *junta militar* solution, be the latter of the present Brazil government, nor the current, presumably progressive, Peruvian kind.

4. Victor Alba, ALLIANCE WITHOUT ALLIES, New York, 1965, pp. 108-119. Alba realizes the difficulties of securing this dynamic democratic "mixed economy" capitalistic transitional system which he believes is the only democratic revolutionary hope for Latin America. He writes: "In order that we do not succumb to the temptation of supposing that the Soviet method is the most efficient or that the classic method is the easiest, it is necessary that the democratic, libertarian methods of development be proved easier and more efficient. With oligarchies in power and in the face of conformist middle classes and contented working classes, this appears to be almost impossible. *This is the source of the danger that haunts Latin America today—worse than the military dictatorship or the Communist dictatorship, because it embraces both*," p. 119 (italics added).

5. Chief spokesman for the FAT group was Alfredo Dominquez, secretary general of FAT and a member of the Executive and Permanent Bureau of the CLAT. My conversations with the ORIT side were exclusively with Arturo Jáuregui. Dominquez stated that now Jáuregui was trying to present a new face to the Latin Americans of a more *latino* organization, but he insisted that "ORIT has been left behind by history." He emphasized what he considered to be the importance of the transformance of CLASC to CLAT, namely that now the movement was a much wider all-embracing workers organization making its

appeal to all kinds of workers, applying the term in its broadest sense, including but going far beyond trade unions and an interest in trade unionism. ORIT, despite Jáuregui's efforts to present a new face ("rostro nuevo"), would continue as the puppet of the AFL-CIO hierarchy and American business interests, and it would be left behind by history. Jáuregui stated that the CLASC-to-CLAT change was indicative of an organization that really never had been a trade union movement trying to make the best of its failure as such and striking a posture as a movement with a wide appeal beyond trade unionism. As for CLAT's appeal to so-called workers in the professions, physicians, lawyers, etc., these people for the most part, he said, were in their own professional organizations and whether in or out of such organizations were decidedly not friends of labor. Thus the potential for CLAT among "professional workers," he felt, was negligible indeed. "Perhaps they are seeking the unemployed bull-fighters and undertakers," he quipped.

6. "The First Conference of Workers Education in Latin America" sponsored by ORIT in Mexico City in January 1964 provided a somewhat dramatic instance of Jáuregui's disagreement with his AIFLD friends. Involved was the question of the proposed new ORIT school in Cuernavaca and some U.S. representatives' objection to it on the grounds that it would duplicate work already being conducted in AIFLD. Jáuregui would not be moved by the objections. He made a blunt address speaking his mind on the subject. Some months later in far off Geneva, home of the International Labor Office, after several martinis (which he does not particularly care for) with George Meany, he convinced the AFL-CIO president that Meany should drop his opposition to the Cuernavaca project and as chairman of the Solidarity Fund of ORIT's international parent body, the ICFTU, throw his vital support behind the new school.

7. EL UNIVERSAL, First Section, page 13, November, 9, 1972. Alfredo Dominguez, of CLAT, dismissed this observation of Jáuregui as just so much rhetoric.

8. Interview in Mexico City, December 1972.

9. A good indication of Máspero's formally stated attitude toward the international parent organization is "The WCL Seen From Latin America," in the special issue of LABOR, Numbers 3-4, 1070, Brussels.

10. "The ORIT and the American Trade Unions: A Case of Conflicting Perspectives," in William H. Form and Albert Blum, (eds.) INDUSTRIAL RELATIONS AND SOCIAL CHANGE IN LATIN AMERICA, Gainesville, Florida, 1965. I called upon the American trade union leaders to do the "impossible"—namely to transcend their own values, which I feel is necessary, if they would effectively forward the social progress which they sincerely have been trying to do (according to their lights) in Latin America. In his AMERICAN LABOR AND UNITED STATES FOREIGN POLICY, 1969, New York, Professor Ronald Radosh takes note of my suggestion and then comments that the accommodation called for on the part of American union leaders "is out of

the question (since) American union leaders work in Latin America explicitly for the purpose of building institutions that can forestall social revolution." He continues: "The unions they build are meant to serve as a means by which the State Department can neutralize Latin American working classes who otherwise might work for revolutionary movements," pp. 373-74. I agree that American union leaders and followers are not doing the "impossible." I should have made clear that their actions reflect their conservativism which I had pointed out results from their having "arrived" as respectable members of U.S. society. As indicated in the text here, they appear in a Latin American milieu as poor helpers in the making of social revolution and thus limit the effectiveness of any Latin American labor leader who seeks to bring about a revolution—even by consent. However, I think that Professor Radosh, himself, is wrong in criticizing conservative American unionists for not making social revolutions. He, even more than I, should know that American trade union leaders should not be expected to lead or embrace extreme changes. Furthermore, I strongly doubt if the redoubtable conservative Mr. Meany and his conservative AFL-CIO colleagues are building trade unions of a kind that the State Department wishes, or in other words doing the work that the State Department assigns them. I would feel that the State Department in these matters might be more the agency of the AFL-CIO than vice versa. All of which is not to fault very real value of Professor Radosh's exposé.

11. This, of course, would take some soul-searching on the part of Doherty and others in the AFL-CIO who have primarily seen the future of Latin America as a contest between communism and democracy. Hopefully, Doherty, after the experience of the last decade, has learned that opposition to communism is insufficient to bolster a labor movement that in some meaningful way can be called "free." The lessening of the cold war's tensions, if not its actual demise, now gives people in the AFL-CIO whom Jáuregui respects an opportunity to shift their emphases. Someone will have to convince George Meany not to identify anti-communism with building freedom. Perhaps William Doherty will undertake the job!

12. The respective attitudes of Máspero and Jáuregui today towards communism needs further clarification. Máspero manifests a position which in recent years has been that of many non-Communists in the West, particularly in Western Europe. Ever since the denigration of Stalin in 1956, when most Western Communists learned of Stalinist terrorism for the first time, there has been a turning away from the former subversion which marked communism. Communists have become genuine nationalists and have reduced the former local suspicion and animosity with which they were viewed. They have come to be accepted as legitimate participants in national politics. Máspero and those who follow him feel like those West Europeans and Latin Americans of the left, including the Catholic left, that in light of all the circumstances it is possible, and indeed worthwhile to join with Communists for certain limited objectives.

Communists, for many Latin American non-Communists, never represented the threat to freedom and that presented by the oligarchy too often supported by the United States.

Jáuregui's attitude which is his own and not a result of AFL-CIO contacts, while it has been modified a bit, is one that will make him extremely suspicious of any proposals involving any common action with Communists. Over the years he always took the strong anti-Communist line that began in his *Aprista* youth, long before he met George Meany or Jay Lovestone. Several observers, including the author, who have been critical of allout anti-communism as the primary concern in the interest of freedom in Latin America, include Jáuregui in this criticism. But because of obvious attacks on him by his enemies it must be repeated that he did not come by his views concerning communism through his association with his AFL-CIO friends.

The ORIT leader's basic hard opposition to communism has been modified to some degree. At least, unlike the AFL-CIO high command, he has come to understand the independence from Moscow of some western Communists and the severe differences that exist between the variegated Communist states. (He has specifically mentioned the Italians and Yugoslavs in conversations with the author.) He believes what he sees as the Communist threat in Latin America is today less severe than in the past decade due to Castro's less belligerent actions. Communism, however, he says, must always be viewed with suspicion by any trade union leader professing a belief in freedom. Latin American Communists, according to Jáuregui, may be weak in numbers but they have a discipline, a strategy, and tactics of division and conquest that makes them a threat far beyond what mere numerical strength might seem to indicate.

13. Such a drastic action on Jáuregui's part would be highly unlikely. He wishes the support of the AFL-CIO to continue and he believes in inter-American cooperation. Ever since George Meany withdrew his organization from the ICFTU the question of AFL-CIO affiliation with ORIT a regional organization of the ICFTU has been unanswered. Jáuregui regards ORIT as a "bridge" between the AFL-CIO and the ICFTU. He hopes that the American labor body will return to the ICFTU, and will also sympathetically comprehend the ORIT's future, more Latin American worker-oriented, course.

14. See, for example, Harvey A. Levenstein, LABOR ORGANIZATIONS IN THE UNITED STATES AND MEXICO, Westport, Connecticut, 1971, pp. 235, 239

Bibliography

Bibliography

I. Selected Secondary Works

Books

Alba, Victor. HISTORIA DEL MOVIMIENTO OBRERO EN AMERICA LATINA. Mexico City, 1964.

Alba, Victor. POLITICS AND THE LABOR MOVEMENT IN LATIN AMERICA. Stanford, California, 1968.

Alba, Victor. NATIONALISTS WITHOUT NATIONS. New York, 1968.

Alba, Victor. ALLIANCE WITHOUT ALLIES. New York, 1965.

Alexander, Robert J. LATIN AMERICAN COMMUNISM. New Brunswick, N.J., 1957.

Alexander, Robert J. LABOR RELATIONS IN ARGENTINA, BRAZIL AND CHILE. New York, 1962.

Alexander, Robert. ORGANIZED LABOR IN LATIN AMERICA. New York, 1965.

Baily, Samuel L. LABOR, NATIONALISM, AND POLITICS IN ARGENTINA. Rahway, N.J., 1967.

Burnett, Ben G. POLITICAL GROUPS IN CHILE. Austin, Texas, 1970.

Davis, S.M., and Goodman, L.W. (eds.) WORKERS AND MANAGERS IN LATIN AMERICA. Lexington, Mass., 1972.

D'Antonio, W.V., and Pike, F.B. RELIGION, REVOLUTION AND REFORM. New York, 1964.

Form, W.H., and Blum, A.A. (eds.) INDUSTRIAL RELATIONS AND SOCIAL CHANGE IN LATIN AMERICA. Gainesville, Florida, 1965.

Goulden, Joseph C. MEANY. New York, 1972.

Halperin, Ernst. NATIONALISM AND COMMUNISM IN CHILE. Cambridge, Mass., 1965.

Horowitz, Irving Louis, et. al. (eds.) LATIN AMERICAN RADICALISM. New York, 1969.

Horowitz, Irving Louis (ed.) MASSES IN LATIN AMERICA. New York, 1970.

Landsberger, Henry A. LATIN AMERICAN PEASANT MOVEMENTS. Ithaca, New York, 1969.

Landsberger, Henry A. (ed.) THE CHURCH AND SOCIAL CHANGE IN LATIN AMERICA. Notre Dame, Indiana, 1970.

Levenstein, Harry A. LABOR ORGANIZATIONS IN THE UNITED STATES AND MEXICO. Westport, Conn., 1971.

Lipset, S.M., and Solari, Aldo (eds.) ELITES IN LATIN AMERICA. New York, 1967.

Lodge, George C. SPEARHEADS OF DEMOCRACY. New York, 1962.

Lodge, George C. ENGINES OF CHANGE. New York, 1970.

MacEoin, Gary. REVOLUTION NEXT DOOR. New York, 1971.

Payne, James L. LABOR AND POLITICS IN PERU. New Haven, Conn., 1965.

Poblete Troncoso, M., and Burnett, B.G. THE RISE OF THE LATIN AMER-ICAN LABOR MOVEMENT. New York, 1960.

Radosh, Ronald. AMERICAN LABOR AND UNITED STATES FOREIGN POLICY. New York, 1969.

Romualdi, Serafino. PRESIDENTS AND PEONS. New York, 1967.

Shapiro, Samuel (ed.) INTEGRATION OF MAN AND SOCIETY IN LATIN AMERICA. Notre Dame, Indiana, 1967.

Urrutia, Miguel. THE DEVELOPMENT OF THE COLOMBIAN LABOR MOVE-MENT. New Haven, Conn, 1969.

Veliz, Claudio (ed.) OBSTACLES TO CHANGE IN LATIN AMERICA. New York, 1969.

Wagley, Charles. THE LATIN AMERICAN TRADITION. New York, 1968.

Williams, Edward J. LATIN AMERICAN CHRISTIAN DEMOCRATIC PAR-TIES. Knoxville, Tenn., 1967.

Articles and Pamphlets

Alexander, Robert J. "Labor and Inter-American Labor Relations." ANNALS OF THE AMERICAN ACADEMY OF POLITICAL AND SOCIAL SCIENCE. March 1961.

Alexander, Robert J. "Latin America's Secular Labor Movement as an Instru-ment of Social Change." In D'Antonio and Pike (eds.), RELIGION, REVO-LUTION AND REFORM. New York, 1964.

Barreiro, Julio. "A Latin American Contribution to the Marxist-Christian Dialogue." In D.R. Cutler (ed.), THE RELIGIOUS SITUATION 1969. Boston, Mass., 1969.

Berger, Henry W. "American Labor Overseas." THE NATION. January 18, 1967.

Bonilla, Adolfo. "Trade Union Movements." In Samuel Shapiro (ed.), INTE-GRATION OF MAN AND SOCIETY IN LATIN AMERICA. Notre Dame, Indiana, 1967.

Castillo-Cardenas, Gonzalo. "Christians and the Struggle for a New Social Order in Latin America." In D.R. Cutler (ed.), THE RELIGIOUS SITUATION, 1968. Boston, 1968.

Delmas, Gladys. "Latin Labor's Alarming Christians." THE REPORTER. Febru-ary 25, 1965.

Goldsack, José. "Why a Christian Democratic Labor Organization." AMERICA. January 28, 1967.

Hawkins, Carroll. "The ORIT and the American Trade Unions." In W.A. Form and A.A. Blum (eds.), INDUSTRIAL RELATIONS AND SOCIAL CHANGE IN LATIN AMERICA. Gainesville, Fla., 1965.

Hawkins, Carroll. "The ORIT and the CLASC: A Case of Conflicting Perspectives." INTER-AMERICAN ECONOMIC AFFAIRS. Winter, 1966.

Hawkins, Carroll. "Labor's Relation to Government and Politics in Latin America." WESTERN POLITICAL QUARTERLY. December 1967.

Kurzman, Dan. "Lovestone's Cold War." NEW REPUBLIC. June 25, 1966.

Landsberger, Henry A. "The Labor Elite: Is it Revolutionary? " In Seymour Lipset and Aldo Solari (eds.), ELITES IN LATIN AMERICA. New York, 1967.

Landsberger, Henry A. "International Labor Organization." In Samuel Shapiro (ed.), INTEGRATION OF MAN AND SOCIETY IN LATIN AMERICA. Notre Dame, Indiana, 1967.

Lens, Sidney. "Lovestone Diplomacy." THE NATION. July 5, 1965.

Lens, Sidney. "Labor Between Bread and Revolution." THE NATION. September 19, 1966.

Lodge, George C. "Revolution in Latin America." FOREIGN AFFAIRS. January 1966.

Máspero, Emilio. EL PAPEL DE LOS TRABAJADORES EN LA CONSTRUCCION DEL SOCIALISMO COMUNITARIO. Merida, Venezuela, 1972.

Máspero, Emilio. "Trade Unionism as an Instrument of the Latin American Revolution." In Irving L. Horowitz, et. al. (eds.), LATIN AMERICAN RADICALISM. New York, 1969.

Máspero, Emilio. "Latin America's Labor Movement of Christian Democratic Orientation as an Instrument of Social Change." In D'Antonio and Pike (eds.), RELIGION, REVOLUTION AND REFORM. New York, 1964.

Máspero, Emilio. LA PRIMERA CONFERENCIA SINDICAL PARA EL DESARROLLO Y LA INTEGRACION DE AMERICA LATINA (Remarks) PODER SINDICAL, FONDO LATINO AMERICANO DE CULTURA POPULAR. Febrero de 1969.

Máspero, Emilio. "The WCL Seen From Latin America." LABOR. Numbers 3-4, Brussels, 1970.

Meisler, Stanley. "Meddling in Latin America." THE NATION. February 10, 1964.

Williams, Edward J. "The Emergence of the Secular Nation-State and Latin American Catholocism." COMPARATIVE POLITICS. January 1973.

Windmuller, John P. "Labor: A Partner in American Foreign Policy." ANNALS OF THE AMERICAN ACADEMY OF POLITICAL AND SOCIAL SCIENCES. November 1963.

II. Documents

U.S. Congress Senate Committee on Foreign Relations. SURVEY OF THE ALLIANCE FOR PROGRESS. LABOR POLICIES AND PROGRAMS. A Study Prepared for the Subcommittee on American Republic Affairs, 90th Congress 2nd Session, July 15, 1968.

VI CONGRESSO LATINO AMERICANO DE TRABAJADORES. 21 al 27 de Noviembre de 1971. (ESTRATEGIA Y POLITICA) III. Caracas. (CLAT).

III. Periodicals

AMERICAN FEDERATIONIST
CLASC
FOREIGN AFFAIRS
LABOR (WCL)
NEW REPUBLIC
NATION
THE AIFLD REVIEW
FREE LABOR WORLD (ICFTU)
WORLD TRADE UNION MOVEMENT (WFTU)

IV. Newspapers

NEW YORK TIMES
NEW YORK POST
EL DIA (Mexico City)
EL UNIVERSAL (Mexico City)
EL MERCURIO (Santiago)
EL SIGLO (Santiago)
LABOR PRESS AND INFORMATION (WCL)
AIFLD REPORT
TRADE UNION PRESS (WFTU)
NOTICIARIO OBRERO INTERAMERICANO (ORIT)

Index

Index

137

About the Author

Carroll Hawkins is on the faculty of the Department of Political Science of Michigan State University. He has taught at the University of Minnesota, Oregon State University, and the University of the Andes in Bogota, Colombia. His particular interest is the politics of the labor movements of Latin America and Spain.